Astrological Signs

ASTROLOGICAL
SIGNS

THE PULSE OF LIFE

by Dane Rudhyar

RAVEN
DREAMS
PRESS

Boulder, CO

Published in 2023 by Raven Dreams Press
3980 Broadway Ste. 103 #186
Boulder, CO 80304
www.ravendreamspress.com

Copyright © 1943 David McKay Co.
Copyright © 1970 by Dane Rudhyar
Copyright © 2023 by Leyla Hill

Originally published in 1943, 1970 and 1974 as
"The Pulse of Life: New Dynamics in Astrology."
Published in 1978 by Shambhala Publications, Inc. as
"Astrological Signs: The Pulse of Life."
Reprinted in 2023 by Raven Dreams Press.

All rights reserved. No part of this publication may be reproduced or transmitted in any form or by any means, electronic or mechanical, including mimeographing, recording, taping, scanning, via internet download, or by any information storage and retrieval systems, without permission in writing from Raven Dreams Press.

Reviewers may quote brief passages.
ISBN 978-1-7326504-8-0

Cover art by Simon Avery
Printed in the United States of America
LCCN (1970) 77-90880

Much of the material incorporated in this book was originally printed in the form of articles in the magazine HOROSCOPE and is revised and expanded here.

To Marc Edmund Jones

TABLE OF CONTENTS

1. The Zodiac as a Dynamic Process 1

2. Twelve Phases of Human Experience 25

    ARIES 25
    TAURUS 34
    GEMINI 42
    CANCER 50
    LEO 58
    VIRGO 66
    LIBRA 76
    SCORPIO 84
    SAGITTARIUS 92
    CAPRICORN 101
    AQUARIUS 110
    PISCES 119

3. The Creative Release of Spirit 129

Chapter One

The Zodiac as a Dynamic Process

THESE are days when all set entities and even the most material of objects are seen dissolving into the dynamic fluency of the new world summoned before our minds by the magic of scientific revelations. From the most common chair, on which we used to sit unaware of the electro-magnetic waves playing within its mass, up to the realm of the human personality, now intricately analyzed into drives and complexes, wherever our mind seeks to know reality it meets the modern emphasis upon rhythmic activity, wave-motion and electro-magnetic interplay of polar energies. Whereas our ancestors used to dwell in a comfortably static universe in which everything has a well-defined and rationally reassuring name, a form and a permanent set of characteristics, today we find change enthroned everywhere. No moment is too small to be analyzed into component phases and events; no object to minute to escape fragmentation and resolution into mysterious somethings which turn out half the time to be electrical charges in a strange game of hide-and-seek.

Against the classical concepts of permanence and identity the realization that all living is a dynamic process of transformation from which no entity escapes now stands backed up by the whole edifice of scientific research and theory. On the ruins of the world of thought dogmatically extolled by nineteenth century minds we witness the reappearance of ancient concepts which were for millennia the foundations of human knowledge. The universe is once more to be understood as an ocean of energies in which two vast complementary tides can be distinguished. Everywhere a dynamic and electrical dualism appears as the foundation upon which all reality stands.

We are very close indeed to the ancient concepts of the ebb and flow of universal Life, of the in- and out-breathings of the universal Brahma. We are practically on the same ground as the Sages of China, who described in their great "Book of Transformations," the *I Ching*, the cyclic waxing and waning of two universal forces of opposite polarities, *Yang* and *Yin*. Likewise, modern thinking has come surprisingly near to some of the most fundamental concepts of ancient astrology; at least when these concepts are seen, not in the light of the classical European mentality, but in terms of a philosophy of human experience. It must be a philosophy of dynamic change if it is a philosophy of human experience, because all that man does experience is a sequence of transformations bounded by birth and death.

It is because astrology can be seen as a most remarkable technique for the understanding of the life-process of change in so many realms — and theoretically in every field — that its renaissance during the last two decades in the Western world is particularly important as a sign of the times. But this importance is conditioned upon a grasp of astrology which is truly modern. Nineteenth century approaches and classical or medieval biases should be discarded in the light of the new twentieth century understanding of physics and above all of psychology, in astrology as in every realm of thought. The emphasis should once more be placed on human experience, and away from the transcendent categories and the mythological entities belonging to an ideology which today is, in the main, obsolete.

Astrology was born of the experience of order made manifest in the sky to primitive man immersed in the jungle and bewildered by the chaos of life on the prolific and wild surface of this planet. The search for order is one of the basic drives in man. At a later stage of evolution this search becomes intellectualized into science; but it has deep organic and instinctual roots.

Instinct is an adaptation to, and an expression of, the periodical order of natural phenomena. It is based on unconscious expectability; and when the normal expectancy of life-circumstances is violently disturbed — as when a college psychologist conducts a certain kind of experiment with white mice or pigs — the animal becomes insane. He is unable to stand the pressure of external disorder upon the internal order of his biological functions, and the latter themselves become disordered.

The constant effort of civilization can be interpreted as an attempt to bring man's understanding of his sense-experiences to the point where the same basic quality of order which he feels in his own organism is seen operating effectively in what appears to him as the outer world. Such an attempt may be called an anthropomorphic illusion by the modern thinker, but why it should be so can never be proven or made convincing to anyone realizing that man can never know anything save what man (collectively and individually) experiences.

Man's experience is originally dual. He feels organic order within as such an absolute imperative that the slightest organic disturbance causes the most acute feeling of pain. Yet man also experiences what seems to him as chaos outside. All sorts of names have been given to this chaos, either to explain it away (as, for instance, Darwin's struggle for life, survival of the fittest, etc.), or to transfigure it into some kind of organic order (vitalistic philosophies), or to interpret it as one pole of a whole, the other pole of which is a noumenal world of archetypes, perfect Ideas and the like (as when the Hindus called it *maya*). Every philosophical system, every religion, every science, every act and every pattern of social organization is only one thing: an attempt to explain disorder and to reconcile it with man's inner organic order.

Astrology is one of these attempts, the most ancient perhaps, or at least the one which has kept its vitality intact for the longest time, because the dualism of celestial order and terrestrial disorder is a universal and essential fact of human experience everywhere. In the sky, all events are regular, periodical, expectable within very small margins of irregularity. On the earth-surface (be it the primordial jungle, the countryside of medieval eras or the modern metropolis) there is relative chaos, unpredictable emotions, irrational conflicts, unexpected crises, wars and pestilence. Astrology is a method by means of which the ordered pattern of light in the sky can be used to prove the existence of a hidden, but real, order in all matters of human experience on the earth-surface.

It not only proves order by relating types, categories and sequences of events to the periods of celestial bodies (as moving points of light – and nothing else), it shows how events can be predicted and how fore-knowledge may be applied in social and personal matters. Fore-knowledge is the power to build a civilization out of the apparent chaos of earthly phenomena. All science is based on predictability. Astrology is the mother of all sciences, the mother of civilization; for it has been the first and the most universal attempt by man to *find the hidden order behind or within the confusion of the earthly jungle — physical or psychological, as the case may be.*

Two Approaches to Life

There are two essential ways in which the dualism of celestial order and earthly jungle can be interpreted in terms of meaning and purpose. The first — the simpler and still the most popular — is to consider the realm of the sky as that of positive, inherently ordered, energizing and eventually controlling Powers which exert a constant *influence* upon the passive, receptive, inert and inherently chaotic (separative) realm of earthly activities, impulses, desires and passions. The sky realm becomes thus the "world of Ideas," or as medieval philosophers called it *Natura naturans*: active Nature, in contradistinction to *Natura naturata*, passive and earthly nature. "Human nature" in such a conception almost unavoidably acquires a pejorative meaning. It is seen as perverted by the "original sin," requiring control by the will of celestial Powers and the reason of divine Intelligences, or to be redeemed by the sacrifice and compassion of a starry being — a "son of God."

Most religious and even classical philosophies have been based on such an interpretation featuring a quasi-absolute dualism of good and evil, spirit and matter, God and nature, reason and emotions, "higher" and "lower." The catastrophic state of Western humankind in our time is the result of such an interpretation which for centuries divided human experience in two parts fundamentally irreconcilable in spite of the efforts of human will and the sacrifice of divine love.

A different type of interpretation is possible, and at times has been attempted. Modern thinkers, from psychologists to physicists, are more than ever striving to build it on solid grounds; but as a more mature mentality is required to grasp its full implications, it is not yet popular, even among trained thinkers steeped in the old tradition of dualistic philosophy and in its transcendent escapes into idealism and absolute monism.

According to this "new" interpretation there is no opposition between the realm of celestial order and that of earthly chaos, because earthly chaos is merely an appearance or fiction. There is order everywhere, *but man is blind to it while he is passing from one type of order to the next and more inclusive type*. What he feels as chaos on the earth-surface is the result of his incomplete vision. When unable to apprehend the wholeness of a situation, man sees it as chaotic – as a jigsaw puzzle whose pieces are lumped into incoherent blocks. The picture cannot be seen while such a condition prevails. There can be only apparent chaos unless every piece is fitted to every other piece in the relationship which the "Image of the whole" determines and to which this Image alone gives meaning.

A human being, considered as a physiological organism, is an ordered whole. What we have called "internal order" is order within the closed sphere of the body — or of the generic nature; man, as a member of the genus, *homo sapiens*. This is the "lesser whole," the lesser sphere of being — and as long as it is not fundamentally disturbed by the pull toward identification with a "greater whole" or greater sphere of being, there is order and organic integration.

However, this state of lesser integration and narrow inclusiveness is never completely undisturbed. The "lesser whole" operates constantly *within* a "greater whole," and there is therefore a ceaseless interaction between the lesser and the greater. *This interaction appears to the "lesser whole" as disorder and is felt as pain. It is seen by the "greater whole" as creative cyclic activity and is felt as sacrifice.* What we call "life" is this constant interaction and interpenetration of "lesser wholes" and "greater whole." It is the substance of human experience; and human experience must necessarily be twofold or dualistic because human experience is always partly the experience of an individual and partly the experience of a collectivity.

The individual feels pain; but also, as he tries to explain it to himself or to some friend, he uses words. His feeling is individual; but his words (and the thinking which has conditioned their formation and their standardized use) are collective. Pain is individual as an immediate experience; but tragedy is social, because it involves a reference to collective values. In every phase of experience, the individual and the collective factors interpenetrate each other. This "con-penetration" is life itself. It is reality.

Instead of two fundamentally separate realms of nature — one celestial, ordered and good; the other earthly, chaotic and dark with sin — we are now dealing with human experience as a whole and analyzing it into two phases. Man experiences what seems to him as jungle chaos and what seems to him as celestial order. In the first case we have human experiences conditioned by the pain felt by the "lesser whole" when relating itself in nearness and immediacy to other "lesser wholes," in the slow process of identifying its consciousness with that of the total being of the "greater whole" — the universe. In the second case, we have human experience when man is relating himself distantly, and through collective observations formulated into laws, with the "greater whole" — or with as much of it as he can encompass.

In both cases experience is one and fundamentally indivisible. We divide it *by establishing two frames of reference*; that is, by lumping together all painful, individual-centered, near experiences into one category — and all inspiring, remote, collectively integrated experiences into another category. We have thus two categories or classes. Each class refers to one *direction* of experience; yet both classes deal with human experience as a whole.

Every human experience is bi-polar. It is pulled by the attraction of the individual factor in experiencing, and also by that of the collective factor. These two pulls are of varied relative strengths. Education (a collective factor) gives more strength to the collective aspect of experience; thus, an educated man may not go as wild under the stress of emotional disturbance as an uneducated person who will kill if jealousy possesses him. But the strongly individualized artist may lose his emotional balance faster than the businessman who is steeped in social respectability. To the Romantic artist the world at large may appear thus as a grandiose tragedy; but the English gentleman will drink his tea while the Empire crumbles, unconcerned to the last moment with the impact of chaos.

From the point of view which has been described in the above paragraphs the substance and foundation of all is human experience. Every valuation is referred to it. All dualisms are *contained within it*. The sky is one aspect of human experience; the jungle, another. The Sage whose life is ordered and at peace, and whose love includes all forms of relationships possible to man (as today constituted), is a "lesser whole" who has reached a kind of integration sustained and measured by the organic order of the "greater whole." He is at peace with himself, because the peace of the "greater whole" is within him. He is at peace with other men, because his relationships to them are, in his consciousness, expressions of, and contained in his relationship to the "greater whole." They fit into a universal picture. Each piece of the jigsaw puzzle is where it belongs. The image of the whole is clear. There is no longer any question of the existence of chaos.

Chaos is the path to a greater wholeness of being and consciousness: a path, a transition, a process. The Sage is he who, first of all, understands this process, feels its rhythm, realizes the meaning of its polar attractions and repulsions. He is the man who sees all nature as a cyclic interplay of energies between "lesser wholes" and "greater wholes." Within him as without, he witnesses individual pain transforming itself into collective peace, and collective fulfillment sacrificing itself into the inspiration and guidance which those who are identified with the "greater whole" can bestow upon "lesser wholes" still struggling with the problems of their atomistic and painful relationships.

A cyclic interplay of polar energies: in this phrase can be found the key to an interpretation of human experience which does not produce irreconcilable dualities and the ever-present possibility of schizophrenia and nationalistic or class wars. Life is a cyclic interplay of polar energies. Every factor in experience is always present, but it manifests in an ever-varying degree of intensity. The waning of the energy of one pole within the whole of experience is always associated with the waxing in strength of the other pole. Two forces are always active. Every conceivable mode of activity is always active within any organic whole, but some modes dominate, while others are so little active as to seem altogether inexistent. Yet non-existence is a fiction, from our point of view. It should be called instead *latency*. No characteristic trait in the whole universe is ever totally absent from the experience of any whole. It is only latent. And latency is still, in a sense, activity of a sort. It is a negative, introverted kind of activity.

Such a philosophical approach to the problem of experience gives to astrology a meaning and a value which few contemporary thinkers suspect it to contain. Astrology can be seen, in the light of this world-philosophy, as a remarkable tool for the understanding of human experience considered as the field for a cyclic interplay of polar energies or attitudes. Astrology is a means to see human experience as an organic whole, a technique of interpretation, an "algebra of life." It uses the ordered pageant of planets (and to a lesser extent, of the stars) as a symbol of what can happen to a man who sees life whole. Every event in the experience of that man is part of an ordered sequence, as every piece of the jigsaw puzzle is part of a complete picture and — because of this, it acquires *meaning*.

It is not that the planets "influence" directly any particular person by flashing a special kind of a ray which will make the person happy or cause him to break his leg. The cycles of the planets and their relationships represent to man reality in an ordered state and in reference to the "greater whole" which we know as the solar system. Men are "lesser wholes" within this "greater whole." Men can only find peace and lasting integration as they relate themselves in consciousness to the "greater whole," as they identify their own cycles of experience with cycles of activity of the "greater whole," as they refer their meetings with other men to the total picture which only a perception of the "greater whole" can reveal. Every man is a whole — an individual. But to be an individual is meaningless except in reference to human society — or at the limit, to the universe. A man living on a desert island without any possibility of his ever being related to another man is not an individual, but only a solitary organism without meaning in terms of humanity. An individual is an individualized expression of collective (or generic) human nature. What he receives from the collective which existed before him, he must return to the collective which follows after him. No individual exists in a vacuum. There is no organic entity which is not contained within a "greater whole" and which does not contain "lesser wholes." To be an individual is a social status. Every man is in latency a universal — or, as the Chinese said, a "Celestial." To bring out the latent into actuality, to transfigure the sphere of earthly man with the light, the rhythms and the integrated harmony which is of the "greater whole" and which the movements of celestial bodies conveniently picture — this is the goal for man.

Astrology opens to us a book of universal pictures. Each picture is born of order and has meaning. Every astrological birth-chart is a signature of the cosmos — or of God. It is the image of the completed jigsaw puzzle. Man, by understanding such images can fulfill his experience, because he can thus see this experience *objectively and structurally as an organic whole*. He can see it as a whole, yet as integrated within the cyclic process of universal change which is revealed clearly in the stars and the planets, and confusedly in the nearness of his earthly contacts. Nothing is static, and no life is absolutely divided. Life is a process, and every process is cyclic — if we believe our experience, instead of imposing intellectual categories and ethical dualisms upon this experience. Astrology is a study of cyclic processes.

The Nature of the Zodiac

All astrology is founded upon the Zodiac. Every factor used in astrology — Sun, Moon, planets, cusps of Houses, nodes, fixed stars, etc. — is referred to the Zodiac. But the Zodiac need not be considered as a thing mysterious, remote and occult. From the point of view above described, the Zodiac is simply the product of the realization by man that experience is a cyclic process; and first of all, that every manifestation of organic life obeys the law of rhythmic alternation — at one time impelled to activity by one directive principle, at another by its polar opposite.

Man acquires first this sense of rhythmic alternation by reflecting upon his daily experience which presents him with a regular sequence of day-time and of night-time, of light and darkness. But human life is too close to such a sequence, and human consciousness too involved in it, for it to appear as anything save a kind of fatality. It does so, because man normally does not keep conscious through the whole day-and-night cycle. He is confronted by a dualism which seems to him absolute, because it is not only a dualism of light and darkness but one which, from the point of view of consciousness, opposes being to non-being. Thus, man is led to use this day-and-night cycle as a symbol to interpret the even greater mystery of life and death. The concept of reincarnation is nothing but a symbolic extension of the original experience common to all men of a regular alternation of days and nights; and so is the ancient Hindu idea of the "Days and Nights of Brahma," of cosmic periods of manifestation followed by periods of non-manifestation — *manvantaras* and *pralayas*.

The cycle of the year, particularly manifest in the seasonal condition of vegetation in temperate climates, offers to man's consideration an altogether different kind of regular sequence. There is no longer any question of one half of the cycle being associated with the idea of absolute non-existence. Man remains active, as an experiencer, through the entire cycle. Indeed, the year can be interpreted as a "cycle of experience" because the experiencer is experiencing through the whole of it — whereas the day-and-night cycle is not normally susceptible of such an interpretation, because during a large portion of it man ceases to be an experiencer.

The Zodiac is the symbolization of the cycle of the year. It is so, essentially, in the temperate regions of the Northern hemisphere where astrology was born. Zodiacal symbolism is the product of the experience of human races living in such regions: experience of the seasons, of the activities of nature and of man through the changing panorama of vegetation — vegetation being the very foundation of animal and human life on earth. As such races have been, during the last millennia, the *active* factor in the evolution of human consciousness, their experience has come to acquire a universal validity in the determination of cosmic meaning and human purpose. Civilization, as we know it today, is therefore centered in a Northern-hemisphere and temperate-climate kind of consciousness. It may conceivably not remain so in the future, but for the time being it is; and our present astrology interprets thus accurately its cyclic evolution.

The Zodiac, which is used in our astrology, has very little, if anything at all, to do with distant stars as entities in themselves. It is an ancient record of the cyclic series of transformations actually experienced by man throughout the year; a record written in symbolic language using the stars as a merely convenient, graphic way of building up symbolic images appealing to the imagination of a humanity child-like enough to be more impressed by pictures than by abstract and generalized processes of thought. The essential thing about the Zodiac is not the hieroglyphs drawn upon celestial maps; it is not the symbolical stories built up around Greek mythological themes — significant as these may be. It is the human experience of change. And for a humanity which once lived very close to the earth, the series of nature's "moods" throughout the year was the strongest representation of change; for the inner emotional and biological changes of man's nature did correspond very closely indeed to the outer changes in vegetation.

Humanity, however, has been evolving since the early days of Chaldea and Egypt. Such an evolution has meant basically one thing and one thing only: the translation, or transference, of man's ability to experience life significantly *from the biological to the psycho-mental level*. At first, humankind drew all its symbols and the structure of its meanings from biological experience. Man, experiencing life and change essentially as a bodily organism, sought to express his consciousness of purpose and meaning in terms of bodily experience. These terms were the only available common denominator upon which civilizations could be built. Even so-called "spiritual" teachings (for instance, the early forms of Yoga or Tantra in India) stressed sexual, and in general "vitalistic," symbols — and corresponding practices.

Progressively, however, leaders among men have sought to center their experience and the experience of their followers around a new structure of human integration: the individual ego. Thus, the need has arisen for translating all ancient techniques of integration and their symbols into the new language of the ego — an intellectual and psychological language. It is because of this need that astrology came into relative disfavor and was replaced by Greek science, logic and psychology as a commanding power in Western civilization. The language of the ego features rationalistic connections and analysis; and in his eagerness to develop the new function of "rigorous thinking," Western man has tried in every way to repudiate or undervalue all organic experiences and all techniques which had enabled his ancestors to give cyclic meaning to their life and to deal with life-situations as wholes of experience. Transcendent idealism broke man's experience in two and created the fallacious opposition of soul and body.

Yet an "occult" tradition kept alive throughout the cycle of European civilization. It tried to re-interpret the symbolism of astrology, and of similar techniques of human integration, at the psychological level. Alchemy and Rosicrucianism were outstanding examples of such an attempt, which had to be veiled in secrecy because of the opposition of the Church. A bio-psychological kind of astrology developed in obscure ways, in which four functions of the human psyche answered to the four seasons of the year and the symbolism of the Gospel became mixed with that of "pagan" lore. And all the while the old traditional forms of astrology, as codified by Ptolemy, kept in use, but mostly as a means to satisfy the curiosity of individuals and the ambition of princes or kings.

Today the remarkable rise to public attention of modern psychology offers to astrologers an opportunity for reformulating completely astrology and its symbols. Astrology can be made into a language, not of the individual ego, but of the total human personality. And, in a world rent with conflicts and made meaningless by the passion for analysis and differentiation at all costs, astrology can appear once more as a technique enabling man to grasp the meaning of his experience as a whole: physiological and psychological experience, body and psyche, collective and individual. Without fear of persecution — it is to be hoped — astrology can use the old vitalistic symbols of ancient astrology, the images derived from the serial changes in the yearly vegetation and from man's experiences with the powers latent in his generic and bodily nature.

These images are rich with the meaning of feelings and sensations common to all men since the dawn of civilization on Earth. They are steeped in collective wisdom

THE ZODIAC AS A DYNAMIC PROCESS 17

and organic instinct. They belong to the Root-nature of man, to "Man's common humanity," the foundation upon which the later-date individual achievements of a rational and over-intellectualized humanity are built. Without the sustaining power of that Root-foundation man must ever collapse and disintegrate. And the very spectacle of such a collapse and disintegration is before our eyes in these dark days of humankind — days nevertheless pregnant with the seed of a new integration of human experience.

It is the purpose of this book to integrate in a brief and suggestive, rather than exhaustive and didactic, manner the ancient symbolism of the Zodiac with the basic images and concepts which have been produced of late, especially by progressive psychologists. Our hope in so doing is that men may be helped to meet more consciously, and as a whole, the integral experience born of our stressful civilization. They can do so, particularly if they cease to think in terms of static categories and set systems, in terms of entities being *either* one thing *or* another; if they begin to face the universe of their experience with other men and all living things as a "greater whole" in which they are ready to participate; if they succeed in having the vision of an integrating and integral evolutionary Purpose in which they may fit their lives jigsawed by the meaningless ambition of being different at all costs.

What the study of the Zodiac will teach us is, first of all, that, while there are always two forces in operation in every situation and in every experience, understanding and decision are never a matter of "either-or," but of "more or less." There is dualism; but the dualism of a dynamic process in which both opposites constantly interpenetrate and transform each other. Because of this, no entity and no experience is either good or bad, constructive or destructive, light or dark. Everything is in everything. What changes is the proportion in which the combination occurs.

In order to understand what the combination is, and to be able to give it a valid meaning, the several components of every experience must be measured. They can be measured in terms of their relative *place* within the boundaries of the whole. They can be measured in terms of their relative *intensity*; and the intensity of any factor depends mostly upon the moment of its cycle at which it operates — whether it represents the "spring" or "winter" of that cycle, whether it is young or old, in its waxing or waning phase, etc.

By enthroning the "more or less" concept in the place of the "either-or" man can completely renew his attitude to life. An experience which, in the mind of the experiencer, *is* good and *is not* bad leads only to conflict and to bondage. If understood as a combination of *more* light *than* darkness, the experience can be referred to the entire cycle in which the two forces, light and darkness, are constantly interacting. The whole cycle can thus be seen at the core of the partial experience; and man can operate as creator of meaning — for meaning resides in the whole, not in any single part.

Every phase of the zodiacal process — every Sign of the Zodiac — represents a state of human experience in which more or less of two basic forces are active. These forces, universal and protean as they are, can be given any number of names. Here, however, because of our attempt to reformulate astrology in terms of the simplest common denominator of *human* experience, we shall refer to these two cosmic forces in constant interplay throughout the year-cycle as the "Day-force" and the "Night-force." Such names not only concur with the most ancient terminology of astrology, but they are natural and logical expressions of the fact that during one half of the year the length of the days increases and the length of the nights decreases correspondingly; the reverse process taking place during the other half of the year. It follows that when the days grow longer the Day-force, the positive tide of solar energy, is on the increase; whereas when the days grow shorter and the nights longer, the Night-force is becoming more powerful while the Day-force wanes in power.

Whenever there are two forces alternately waxing and waning in relative strength, four critical, basic moments must of necessity be found. Thus:

1. At the winter solstice (Christmas) the Day-force is at its weakest and the Night force at its strongest level. This is the beginning of the Zodiacal Sign: *Capricorn*.
2. At the spring equinox (around March 21) the Day-force which has increased in strength while the Night-force decreased, equals in power that Night-force. Zodiacal Sign: *Aries*.
3. At the summer solstice (around June 21) the Day-force reaches a maximum energy, the Night-force its lowest ebb. Zodiacal Sign: *Cancer*.
4. At the fall equinox (around September 21) the two forces are again equal, the Night-force having grown stronger ever since the beginning of the summer. Zodiacal Sign: *Libra*.

In studying a cyclic process, the first difficulty encountered is that of determining the starting point of the cycle. In ultimate philosophical analysis there is no starting point, yet for practical purposes the mind must select a beginning in order to interpret significantly the process in terms of human experience. This selection of a starting point establishes a "frame of reference"; and it is not to be considered, in any sense, a haphazard selection. *The selection is imposed upon the experiencer by the meaning which he gives to his experience of the cyclic process.*

From the point of view of physical experience with nature — "human" or otherwise — and as long as the Zodiac is considered as a dynamic process of change, it is clear that one of the four climactic points above defined should logically be selected as the beginning of the cycle. Moreover, in a philosophy which does *not* give a basically higher valuation to any phase of experience at the detriment of the opposite and complementary phase, it is equally evident that it is more befitting to start the cycle at a time when the two forces alternately waxing and waning are of equal strength; thus at one of the equinoxes. The spring equinox has been selected as the beginning of the Zodiac because man naturally identifies his experience, first, with the realm of growing things and sunlight, and only later with the more hidden realm of values which the seed and winter life symbolize. The spring equinox in the temperate regions of the Northern hemisphere is what astrologers call the "first point of Aries" — and we have seen that the roots of our civilization are to be found in these regions which are the cradle of our astrology.

THE ZODIAC AS A DYNAMIC PROCESS

The Day-force and the Night-force

One cannot understand significantly the beginning of any cycle unless one knows the general meaning of the whole cycle. By the very definition of the term "cycle," the beginning of a cycle marks also the end of the preceding one. Beginning is conditioned by end, as the new vegetation is conditioned by the seeds which were the product of the preceding yearly growth. To know the general meaning of a cycle is to know the nature of the two basic forces which are at play throughout its course. We must therefore define, first of all, the characteristics of the Day-force and the Night-force; and our definitions will center around concepts of a psychological nature, because it is the purpose of this book to establish astrological factors at the new level at which modern man is now consciously and deliberately operating: the psycho-mental level.

The Day-force is a *personalizing* energy. It forces ideas, spiritual entities, abstractions into concrete and particular actuality. It energizes the "descent of spirit into a body" to use a familiar, though dangerous, terminology. Thus, it begins to grow in power at the winter solstice, symbol of spiritual Incarnation; but becomes only clearly visible in Aries, symbol of germination — and in humans, of adolescence. It is fulfilled in Cancer, symbol of "coming of age" and of personal fulfillment through marriage or home-responsibilities. The natural result of the action of the Day-force is the stressing of that individual uniqueness of human being which is known today as "personality."

The Night-force is an *in-gathering* energy. It brings personalities together. First, in Cancer (the home) it integrates the couple intent on starting a family; in Leo, it adds the child; in Virgo, the helpers, nurses, educators. But integration becomes public only in Libra, the symbol of social activity, of group activity toward the building of a cultural and spiritual community. With Scorpio, business and political enterprises flourish; with Sagittarius, philosophy, printing, long journeys. The Night-force reaches its apex of power with Capricorn, symbol of the State — the organized social whole. The natural result of the action of the Night-force is to emphasize all values related to "society."

Personality and Society — such are, indeed, the two polarities of the actual experience of human beings ever since we can trace our historical development. The two terms are the *concrete* manifestations, at the psychological level, of the two still more general concepts of "individual" and "collective." In every human experience these two factors are present with varying relative strengths. That this is so should never be forgotten. No person acts and feels solely as an individualized personality, or solely as a social being. It is never a question of "either-or" but of "more-or-less." It is a matter of point of view.

In a somewhat similar manner, we may speak of our Sun as a "sun" or as a "star." It is a "sun" if considered as the center of an individualized and separate cosmic organism (a solar system); but it is a "star" if considered as a participant in the collective being of the Galaxy. In the first case, he is alone on his throne; in the second case, he is constantly related to his fellow-stars within the boundaries of the "greater whole," the Galaxy. Man experiences the Sun as light-giver — as a "sun" — during daytime. At night, modern man realizes that this giver of light, this All-Father, is but one "star" in the companionship of the Galaxy. Overcome by light and heat, we worship the "sun" in devotion; in the silence and peace of the night we commune with the brotherhood of "stars." It is the same reality always, but we change our angle of approach to it — and the one reality divides into two phases of experience, and again into many more phases. The limit to the divisibility of our experience is only our ability to remain integrated as a person under this process of differentiation — our ability to remain sane; which is, to give an integral meaning to our experience as a *social personality*.

The dualism of personality and society becomes in another and more strictly psychological sense that of "conscious ego" and "Collective Unconscious." The realm of individualized consciousness is the realm of day-time, the realm of "sun." The realm of the Collective Unconscious is the night-realm, the realm of "stars." An understanding of these two realms is necessary in order to see how the waxing and waning of the two cyclic forces operate in a psychological manner.

To say simply that the Day-force begins to wane after the summer solstice does not give an accurate psychological picture of what happens within the human person. It is not only that the Day-force becomes less strong. More accurately still, the waning of the Day-force means that what was a positive, active force is becoming more and more withdrawn from the field of objectivity. *It becomes increasingly subjective and introverted; also, more transcendent.* It operates from the point of view of unconscious motives, rather than from that of conscious ones.

Human experience is not only to be referred to consciousness and to the individual ego; for, if we do so, we have to give an ethical valuation to many of our experiences, which divides our total being into two conflicting entities. Thus, some of our acts may have to be explained as proofs of our evil personality, others as manifestations of our heroic or saintly individuality; they *must* be given such interpretations if they are referred *only* to the conscious ego. But if we realize that our actions are partly the results of conscious endeavors, and partly the products of motivations emerging from an unconscious which is not "ours" (in an individualized way) but which is an ocean of racial and social energies unconcerned with ego structures, ethics and reason — then we can explain human actions in another way; and man may know himself integral and undivided, a center of universal Life in its process of cyclic change.

From such a point of vantage man can see consciousness constantly interpenetrating unconsciousness, rationality rhythmically playing with irrationality — and not be disturbed, or frantically striving to be what he is not. Human experience is forever the outcome of this interplay of consciousness and unconsciousness, of individual and collective. Cyclic life pulsates through every human action, feeling or thought. Reality has a rhythmic heart. The systole and diastole of that heart create these beats of becoming which are birth and death, winter and summer, increase of light and crescendos of darkness. Gloriously, the dance of experience moves on in the hallways of nature's cycle. The Sage looks on, yet every phase of the dance pulsates through his awareness. He is spectator, yet he is partner to all protagonists in the universal dance; every lover knows him as beloved, and his mind experiences the throb of every human heart. His vision encompasses all birthing and dying. Upon all things born of the pulsing and the dancing of cyclic Life, he bestows Meaning. And in that bestowal of Meaning, Man, total and free, creates reality.

Chapter Two

Twelve Phases of Human Experience

ARIES

PIERCING through the crust of the soil which the melting of snow softened, the sprouting seed forces its life into the light of the sun. The fervent upreaching of spring brings forth the wonder of germination. The Day-force now balances in intensity the waning Night-force. The player who leaves the stage will soon be but a memory, however potent this memory may be in the recesses of the human psyche. The new star asserts his right before the footlights of the human consciousness. Henceforth, the show will be his. Yet, his voice is unassured; his countenance reveals hidden fears in its very bravado. In Aries the human personality experiences its phase of adolescence.

Until puberty comes to the growing child, the horizon of personality is mapped by the walls of some enclosing matrix. First, the mother's womb; then, the more diversified space of the family, holding within its secure walls increasing conflicts. But, whether bounded by physical or psychological envelopes, the personality of the child is still at the prenatal stage. It is enfolded by collective nature. It struggles to emerge. Emergence — the wonder and the fear of it — is adolescence. The adolescent is born as a separate person in a world which seems hostile or alien; which must be conquered; which must not be feared.

Fear mixed with eager expectancy, awkwardness, emotional confusion — this is the adolescent. He rushes in desire; swiftly recoils at the least hurt. He is bold, in a giggling way. Compelled by an inner necessity to go on, he asserts himself with blatancy and daring; yet he wishes he could withdraw to the security of mother earth. The least wind of fate makes shrink and suffer this "lamb" at heart rushing headlong like a "ram."

This psychological description of adolescence characterizes the basic nature of the Aries type; his emotional instability and his disordinate, fate-compelled desire; his acute sensitiveness masquerading under a "devil-may-care" attitude; his sheer instinctuality and his often bombastic self-assertiveness which is actually not real self-centeredness but rather the outcome of a bio-psychological compulsion deeply and fatefully experienced. The Aries human being is compelled from within to acquire at any cost a self; compelled to force his remote individual soul to assume the burden of incarnation. He does not seek power in order to satisfy himself, but to demonstrate himself to himself — the power necessary for him to become a personality. And if he seems needy for love and fame, for "women, wine and song" it is because he feels weak or uncertain within himself and needs constant reassurance and outer sustainment.

Because in him the Day-force barely overcomes the Night-force, the Aries person has to throw his conscious ego acutely, at times almost desperately, into his will to live — and he often *over*does it. His nostalgia is as great as his impatience; his sentimentality as romantic as his passion is sharp, direct — yet short-lived and subject to fits of revulsion. More than any other zodiacal type he loves his need for love rather than a particular person. And he needs love because he is fundamentally afraid of the world and lonely; yet he is just as fearful of the bondage implied in a permanent union or association, because he must keep growing, he must constantly extend his budding personality, he must at all cost avoid standing still, which would soon mean lapsing into the past. His pioneer instinct is a disguised fear of routine and of the pull of tradition. He *has* to keep growing; and changing partners, changing his horizons and his allegiances gives him at least the sense of moving on, the illusion of growth.

The ordinary Aries type would, of course, deny violently these hidden springs of his actions. He cannot stop moving forward and try to understand himself. He is not building consciousness, but personality. He is no thinker, fundamentally; but rather a builder. He has to exert his urge to live. The Day-force is mounting up within him with phallic intensity. It does not matter what or where he builds. But he must feel himself in movement of destiny. He must feel himself acted upon by great energies.

A formed personality can act slowly, quietly, deliberately; because it acts from a relatively set basis of individual selfhood. But the Aries type is constantly in the process of forming himself. He has no sense of set selfhood; no sense of set boundaries. He is ever open to the inrush of universal, non-personified Life. He is never a finished product, and he cares little for finishing what he attempts.

He is taken up by the act of creating, not by his creations. And therefore, he needs to feel back of him, compelling him to create, more and more Power, more and more Life. All he wants is to dispense this Power to others, the fecundate virgin fields with it — and to pass on, ardent with the impregnating of still vaster and "new" fields.

In that sense he is "im-personal." He is a giver — but not of the things which are "his own." He is a giver of sheer energy, the energy of the Day-force that is bubbling forth in him. It is hard for him to make anything "his own." Yet if he does it, then he clings to that thing (for a while at least) with passion — a passion born of fear and loneliness; because the thing becomes suddenly for him a symbol of his own personality — the personality being actually the only one thing which he craves to "own" and or which he is never sure, for it never can be "finished."

Because in Aries the Day-force and the Night-force balance one another, the Aries person is always in a state of unstable equilibrium, pulled internally by opposites; thus restless, fretful, nervous, often neurotic. But his neuroses are actional ones, born of a sense of failure because of insurmountable obstacles, of weariness before the effort, or lack of *personal* interest in the actions, in the performing of which he may seem all the while to throw great energy or passion. That energy is not actually "his own." He is not in it. He is constantly seeking to fulfill himself as personality; but that goal is ever elusive — always beyond, beyond. And so he keeps acting, desiring, emoting, creating — barely succeeding in covering up by the stress of activity the emptiness and the fear of an eternal adolescence.

No one may know this among his associates. He is not only all taken up by action, but he is also an actor.

He plays parts, and he loves the sense of being directed in his lines by an invisible Playwright; for that gives him a sense of security in his inherent destiny. He can easily become a great devotee; just because he is not sure of his own personality. He has, symbolically, "adolescent crushes" for some "Teacher," into whom he projects his passion for personality. Rather than display a weak personality of his own, he absorbs himself in the devotion to a great Personage — but preferably one that is remote, ideal, absent. This absorption is always a "psychological projection" of his own yearning for personality. If he cannot act by outer show of creativeness and fecundation the part of personality, then be projects that yearning, transforming it in an intense (but often fitful) devotion for an ideal Figure, or for a "great Cause."

In Aries, personality is still not quite separated from the act. It is contained in the direct immediacy of an activity caused by an irrational power which, at one level, is "instinct" and at another "God." Action here is straightforward; yet because a sense of inner insecurity tends to bend down to the soil the adolescent shoot buffeted by social storms, this type of action needs often a prop. The Aries person has, however, to glorify this needed form of sustainment; to make it impersonal, so that his own personality be not weakened in the eyes of others — or in his own eyes. Indeed, he knows, subconsciously if not consciously, what he lacks. He knows that his personality is hardly as yet a concrete fact; that it is only emerging from the subjective state. But this means also that it is as yet rooted in the immensities of the collective life, that it is filled with potency — filled with élan *vital*, with the surging and formative power of universal evolution...which many men have named God.

In Aries, the "pulsing of life" — of the creative Breath — is felt. It passes through. It surges forth — and is gone. Aries power is the power of the lightning, which descends from above, which strikes out of the darkness of the Collective Unconscious. It is the power of revelation; power of Destiny released, which burns and fecundates. Such a power, from whatever level it operates in fiery downflows, gives to the actions of an Aries person a peculiar pioneering, impersonal, perhaps cosmic and fateful strength. Indeed, in and through the noblest expressions of Aries power it is not an individual person who is at work, but humanity — Man. At less exalted levels, a social or religious group, a nation, a race may voice their needs and state the solutions to these needs through such a person — who is not quite a conscious personality and yet much more than an individual.

As such a person senses the meaning of the destiny which through him is becoming, pride may roar through his ego. He may become arrogant. He may make demands upon society, as if all kinds of privileges were his "by divine right." Yet, more often than not, his pride is rather adolescent, mixed with humility and a peculiar feeling of insecurity; for he knows inwardly that he does not own the source of the pride-giving power, that he might lose the contact — and become empty. This differentiates the Aries pride from that typical of Leo; for in Leo, pride is centered in personality and rooted in a glory-seeking "I am." The Aries person will stress the "am" rather than the "I." His pride is in what he does, in what is done through him, in that great force which is at his command, in the powerful masculinity of his organism. It is not essentially in what he personally is; for he is never quite sure of what he is.

Aries is the dawn of personality as an objective and conscious fact in the cycle of human unfoldment. In that dawn the light of consciousness gradually sweeps through the Eastern sky, awakening all forces which belong to the realm of the Day. But there is still darkness in the West. The power of the Night is still holding sway over vast regions of the human psyche. Henceforth it will control the memory and gain possession of the regions below-the-horizon. These regions constitute the Unconscious.

As a man awakens, he meets his dreams — the twilight memory of the Night state of the psyche. Their irrationality haunts his awakenings. And because the pull of the Night-force is still strong and insistent, the Aries person clings with dogmatic or devotional intensity to "ideas," to "reason" and "logic." These are witnesses to the triumph of the Day-force over the irrational phantasms of the realm of Night. They are the bulwarks of form and consistency over chaos and pre-natal fears. But if the Aries person lets go of the conscious and withdraws inwardly, he finds himself well-nigh flooded with the prolific fantasy of his unconscious.

As the turning-point of the spring equinox is passed, the Night-force, overcome by the waxing intensity of the Day-force, leaves the stage of the conscious; but only to become introverted, subconscious or transcendent. We have already shown how this Night-force reaches fulfillment in Capricorn, in the fulfillment of the social-cultural ideal of togetherness — the State. In the two subsequent zodiacal Signs, Aquarius and Pisces, that group-forming urge, that will to build a collective and permanent "greater whole" out of a multitude of personalities, becomes spiritualized, more-than-physical, more-than-social. Thus, Aquarius symbolizes social idealism, social reform, social transformation under the influence of Uranus; and in Pisces we reach the concept of the "invisible Community," and "Church triumphant" — in Heaven; the "Communion of the Saints," symbolized by Neptune.

The Night-force in Aries operates in a still more transcendent manner. Its symbol is the "Lamb slain for the redemption of the world" — in other words, *martyrdom*. In martyrdom the Aries person performs a transcendent type of action, one which is impelled by the great urge he has to live and to reach immortality as a self; for, to be a martyr is to become, in the eyes of society, the immortal symbol of a Cause. It is to be fulfilled in death as a personality.

This is the immortality of the seed, which dies as a seed so that there may be once more life and vegetation. It is the eternal Crucifixion of that which was sown in Libra. The seed dies into the new life, as night and the stars vanish into the glowing sunrise. And that death of night and stars, that death of the seed, haunts the subconscious of the Aries type who is not entirely absorbed in frantic activity and scattered fecundations. Thus, the Aries vision, beyond the threshold of the conscious, yearns for the seed; which is to him, the Mother. While in his conscious nature he acts for the future, subconsciously he dreams of the past.

The balance between conscious and unconscious is very subtle in Aries — and also in Libra. These two signs are signs of equilibrium, in which the Day-force and the Night-force are of nearly identical strength. "Nearly" identical only; because in Aries the Day-force has an outward momentum which assures its domination — but a domination which must pay homage to the past, to the Night-force.

In one sense at least, the Aries person is called upon to sacrifice his past, to burn it on the altar of his dedication to the new life. This sacrifice could be a joyous or serene act; but the power of the Night-force in the subconscious often makes of it a dramatic martyrdom. Thus, the feeling of *self-pity* so often found in Aries people. That self-pity is produced by the ebbing Night-force clinging still to its hegemony. It is a negative characteristic of Aries. Self-pity, weariness before the act, a sense of "what is the use," a sense of being a "sacrificial victim" of destiny — are all negative aspects of that sign. They can only be overcome when the conscious ego succeeds in "assimilating the contents of the Unconscious" (in C. G. Jung's terminology), when all the energies of the Aries type are embodied deliberately and consciously into a work and a destiny, consciously accepted and discharged.

Thus, Aries: its strength and its weakness, its burden of destiny. The song of Aries is a song of solar "exaltation" because in and through it the Sun — "exalted" in Aries — feels for the first time that victory has been won. This victory over the Night is celebrated on the nineteenth degree of Aries, the point of "ecstasy" of the solar force. It is the symbolical Resurrection-day, Easter. Later on, in Leo, the conscious solar ego will realize itself utterly in the joy of creative self-expression; but at Aries 19° the Day-force triumphs with the ebullition of the first love of adolescence. Then Life pours exuberantly into the youth who feels himself dilated into the universe. It is indeed the Easter song of rejoicing — the first blossomings of the trees, before Taurus-green leaves appear.

TAURUS

After having triumphed over the Night-force at the equinox the Day-force which, throughout Aries, rushed forth in adolescent desire for self-manifestation, becomes in Taurus steadier and more persistent. It ceases to fight — often merely against ghosts and windmills — for the privilege of exteriorizing its energy as a personality. It seeks to establish itself in a tangible manner. It demands results; and it learns that results are gained through repetition, through set motions, through stubborn insistence and undeviating effort. It learns, moreover, that only intimate contact with the substance of the earth can bring forth these concrete products, the fruition of which is human personality. In Taurus, therefore, the Day-force is seen acting upon the substantial foundation of all organisms, stirring the soil of humankind into fruitfulness.

Taurus is the reaction which follows Aries action. After the peculiar inner insecurity of Aries, of which the Aries person often makes a challenge and a virtue, Taurus presents the spectacle of an emphasis on security. The pioneering instinct gives way to the settler's organizing faculty. Energy transforms itself into power; this, as sheer ability to move, finds a resistant material into and against which to move. Sheer motion in Aries becomes, in Taurus, emotion aroused by objects. In Aries, universal Life pours through an adolescent ego craving for individual selfhood. In Taurus, the forces of tradition, of habit and of material inertia blend with that selfless, half-conscious outpouring of energy; a rotational movement is produced, whence will grow a definite sense of personality, a limited destiny.

Aries acts in a straight line; Taurus in a circular motion — Gemini will combine both through the spiral. A straight line can always be seen, in geometry, as a tangent to a circle. It shows the action of a force which escapes the bonds of circular motion. Likewise, germination breaks the closed globular unit constituted by the seed. Aries (the germinal up-shoot) is thus release through tangential motion; after which Taurus bends the tangent back to a circular orbit, stopping what otherwise would be a constant exhaustive flow of energy into space: an explosion.

Aries and Taurus are complements. But not in the sense in which Aries and Libra are also complements and polarities. Aries is fundamentally opposed to Libra. The directions of their activities are opposite. Aries is moving toward a maximum Day force; Libra toward an ever-stronger Night-force. On the other hand, both Aries and Taurus are characterized by a mounting Day-force. But in Aries that Day-force is straightforward action, because its main problem is to overcome definitely the Night force. The Night-force, having been definitely overcome, a new need arises: the need for stabilization and voluntary restriction. This is Taurus' work.

In Aries, activity is sought for activity's sake. There is a will to freedom, a fear of bondage, an identification with sheer mobility and the systemless-ness of first conquests. This leads obviously to dispersion and to a peculiar sense of futility, of life flowing like sand through open fingers. Then the need for *coalescing action* arises. Taurus fills that need; not by fundamentally opposing the direction of the Aries Day force, but merely by modifying it through the realization of a new purpose.

The difference between Aries-energy and Taurus-energy is a difference of purposes. The two energies have the same direction. They are indeed only one energy, which after reaching a certain end in Aries, seeks to fulfill a new phase of its development in Taurus. *The purpose of Aries is dynamic; that of Taurus is organic.*

When an acid corrodes a metal somewhere on the surface of the earth, such is a disintegrating, *dynamic* activity. But when the hydrochloric acid in a man's stomach digests proteins, there an *organic* function is operating. In other words, the acid in the stomach fulfills a function in terms of the need of an organic whole, the human body; and its operations are more or less rigidly controlled by that need. On the other hand, free acid will corrode everything it touches. In itself and of itself, it has no particular functional purpose in any definite organic whole.

The Aries type acts; and that action is its own justification. There is a compulsion of Destiny back of it, but the Aries person merely takes it for granted and *his consciousness* is all satisfied by the sheer fact of activity. For the Taurus type action is essentially meaningless without a purpose. It must be related to something. There is in Taurus a compulsion of relationship; in Aries, a compulsion of activity. In Taurus activity must be functional in terms of the organism, the purpose of which it serves.

Sex, for instance, is for the Aries type almost solely a mode of actional release. It is in itself its own justification as a thrill of activity, of projective strength in operation. But for Taurus, sex means the condition for the production of a definite result; normally, a child.

"Production" is a key-word with Taurus. Everything which Taurus touches should be productive if it is at all to be considered as significant. But production depends upon the control of the basic energies of human or earthly nature. Aries seeks only release of energy; Taurus insists on making energy productive. It *puts to use* the Aries energy. Productive energy — energy which is controlled and formed — is power. Thus, Taurus is a power-Sign of the Zodiac. It is one of the four great moments of the year-cycle when life operates definitely and creatively in terms of power and purpose. The fifteenth degree of Taurus is, in relation to the cross formed by equinoxes and solstices, a 45-degree point of the circle — the others being Leo 15°, Scorpio 15°, and Aquarius 15°. These points are gates through which power and purpose are released and experienced. They are "alchemical" points, and, in the Bible, they are symbolized respectively by the Bull, the Lion, the Eagle and the Angel.

Taurus is the "good earth," the bountiful Great Mother; and it can be considered as a feminine Sign. Nevertheless, strangely enough, it is represented in astrological symbolism by the Bull, and not by a female animal. This should make one careful not to overstress the passive or receptive characteristics of this Sign. It is not only a sign of strong ascendancy of the Day-force and a symbol of purposeful determination. It represents that very power which surges from the depths of inchoate substance and constantly seeks to reach the higher level at which the basic awareness in any natural organism can operate. It is the "good earth," but what we name thus is the very thin layer of the earth-surface which is susceptible of bearing a harvest of plants and trees. It is the rich, black soil (a few inches deep perhaps) without which there could be no life on earth.

This surface layer of the earth is the place of meeting for earth-vibrations and sun-radiations. It is there that the fecundation of the earth by the solar force takes place; there that living organisms are born — whether it be in shallow sea-waters or in the humus which forms the thin layer of top-soil. Indeed, all life on our planet is only "skin-deep." Likewise, all our experiences of the outside world are gained through the skin and specialized portions of its surface: the senses. The realm of the conscious is also the topmost layer of the vast Unconscious, and the rational and analytical faculties covered by the term "intellect" are again but the very last, topmost development of human consciousness. The intellect — cream of the conscious faculties which, in turn, are the cream of man's mind or intelligence — will not reveal its real possibilities until Gemini is reached; yet, this Gemini spring-harvest is largely conditioned by the Taurus soil from which it must grow, as well as by the Aries fecundating power which makes that soil fruitful.

Taurus is the phase of life and experience in which the upreaching surge of evolution finds its most concentrated and most vocal expression. It is the fruitful surface of the earth; but that surface seen as the highest level reached by the élan *vital* — and from this surface, plants rise further to meet the sun and perform the alchemy of light. The earth reaches up through its trees whose chlorophyll captures the solar radiations, and, in the leaves, the sun's energy is chemically fixed and *made usable* for further evolution on this planet. Animals eat up the leaves. Tree trunks decompose and become coal. The trees condense the moisture of the air and help in bringing down the fecundant rains; and the rains make rivers and waterfalls — whence electric power is produced.

All power on this earth has its substantial base in the chemical action of the green plants and of their chlorophyll which is nearly identical in chemical nature to the red blood cells. Green and red: two polarities — Taurus and Aries. The former gives energy to living organisms; the latter after a further alchemical process, produces in man conscious thought — for there can be no conscious thinking on earth without red blood. Aries is a divine Visitation, a descent of power; but to Taurus belongs the substance of every new evolutionary progress, for Taurus is the symbol of that power which forever produces new organisms. Taurus' keynote is evolutionary fulfillment from the depths upward.

Because all life-energies rise in Taurus to the surface, pulled by the will-power and desire of the Sun, the individual Taurean finds the source of his power in the racial depths of his unconscious; thus, he identifies himself at root with the race that bore him, while ever striving to attune his conscious sense of purpose to that superior will which directs him from within toward the next stage of his evolution. The outer manifestations of this impersonal, instinctual or cosmic will may be delayed; but they can hardly be stopped.

Thus, the determination, stubborn self-will and fixity of purpose of the Taurus type. These characteristics often lead to a sense of possessiveness. Possessiveness comes as a result of the deep sense of an inner need which *must* be satisfied. Whatever fulfills this need acquires such a value that it seems imperative to the individual to assure its possession. Essentially, the Taurus type will think of the use which a person, a situation or a relationship will be *to him*. Yet this may not mean selfishness, but rather the outcome of the vital realization that a fact of experience cannot have meaning unless it fulfills a definite purpose. Where anything fulfills a functional purpose, there the thing belongs and should stay.

At the Taurus stage, personality is not yet set. But that feeling of usefulness and purposefulness is the foundation upon which a set personality will be built; for personality is an organic concept. Self-sufficiency, at least of a relative kind, is the basis of personality. Taurus provides the sense of self-sustainment, on which self-sufficiency can develop. Thus, the link between Cancer, Sign of rulership of the Moon, and Taurus, in which the Moon is "exalted." The purpose of procreation (Taurus) conditions the building of the home (Cancer). What is needed, however, before the home can be built is to compel the creative energy (Aries) to accept that purpose. This will be the work of Gemini, the weaver of patterns of relationship and of ideals — those nets in which the Aries freedom will be caught.

In Taurus, the Night-force is also operative, but in an even more remote way than in Aries. The fixity of purpose of the Taurus person, gathering outer sustainment to substantiate and actualize the building of personality or home, leaves little room for the attenuated Night-force in the consciousness. But it is still evident in the subconscious or in the relation of the Taurus person to the large vistas of the Collective Unconscious. It manifests as a peculiar intoxication based on the irrational or supra-rational sense of identification with a mystical purpose; on the feeling that one is invested with the power of an invisible community. Thus, the sense of being a Prophet, a Messiah, a Redeemer, an Avatar; a mouthpiece of Divinity.

This can manifest in many small ways, or in a very big way. It may be a delusion. It may be a reality. The fruits alone can prove which of the two hypotheses is the actual one. Taurus is the sign in which the symbolical Pentecost occurs. Men are being invested with transcendent, super-conscious, irrational power. The "gift of tongue" is a symbol of the irrationality, or rather super-rationality, of that power — a particular language being always considered as the perfect symbol of the operation of the rational faculty.

According to tradition, be it symbolical or a literal fact, Gautama the Buddha was born, achieved liberation, and died at the Full Moon of May during the Taurus phase of human experience. The meaning of this is that Gautama can be considered — from the point of view of occult wisdom — as the very "cream" of *human* evolution and the first exemplar of the highest type of consciousness possible to a human being *born of this earth*. Divine Manifestations, before or since him, may have been greater Personages, but if so, it is because they were descents of divine power and not, as Gautama the Buddha, climaxes of human consciousness.

As Gautama taught in India, the constellation of the Pleiades was found at the end of the zodiacal Sign, Aries. Many seers and astrologers of the past have claimed that the Pleiades constitute the center of our universe of human experience. If so, from that center spring everlastingly the Power and the Love that vivify and integrate the entire cycle of our evolution. Indeed, Aries is the symbolical fountain head of manifested life; but Taurus, energized by the Pleiades since the days of Christ, is the steady flowing river whose substance feeds the multitudes with "living waters." On its banks great cities are built; civilization grows and matures; and men seek for the Mystery which is beyond change — which sustains and illumines the whole universe.

GEMINI

With Gemini we come to the last phase of spring experience. The Day-force, which we saw rushing and bubbling in adolescent impetuosity like a mountain stream (Aries), has reached in Taurus the quieter level of plains fruitful with the work of man. The dynamic energy of nature has become organic power — energy put to use and made to assume a function in the economy of living. The adolescent has met his first loves. He has learnt to feel his way and to establish himself as an individual entity among his kin. He has learnt to give a somewhat formed expression to the ancestral forces welling up from his tradition. His now is the task of extending his capacity for human relationship — indeed, for all kinds of relationships, within himself and outside of himself. His whole being now yearns for a vivid extension of the sphere of his experience. Perhaps college life gives him full opportunity to meet many new comrades, to delve into many new kinds of thought, to experience new facets of himself in scattering the energy of his feelings among a multitude of unfamiliar objects and personalities.

The Night-force, at this Gemini stage, reaches its lowest ebb. It represents then the power of the family womb, of collective tradition, of all the subtle ties and habits which cling to the youth eager to emerge from every possible kind of bondage to the past in which he nevertheless has his roots. He refuses, as a rule, to acknowledge such a bondage; yet his buoyant and cocksure feeling of independence is mostly a negative reaction against things which still bind him in his subconscious depths. He gains his illusory freedom *against* the ancestral collectivity; while true liberation is freedom *from* that which has been consciously fulfilled, then dismissed as bondage while retained as substantial sustainment. The power of the Night-force is thus almost entirely negative in Gemini. It is inverted; it energizes more or less subtle psychological complexes which the youth, unaware of their existence, will project unwillingly upon the sensitive plate of his future homelife.

But the youth has no time to bother about complexes or to analyze the manner in which his eager desire to emerge from the set relations of his family life operates. All he seeks to do is to extend into new fields whatever means he has of associating his as yet uncertain sense of personality with a multiplicity of new factors. At the purely biological level, the raw materials of associative activity are impressions, nervous sensations, immediate reactions to impacts reaching the senses and the consciousness. At the level of the mind, remembrance, comparison, analysis, and the formation of mental images to be expressed through words, are phases of an activity which develops the intellect through the use of language. This development is originally contained in the sphere of the near environment and constantly referred to the individual who, through it, relates himself with an ever-increasing number of facets of human nature.

In Gemini we see language in its incipient stage, mind being born with the creative fervor of the Day-force in springtime. We see the poet, the artist in words expressing his self for the sheer joy of building his own personality through the extension and the memorizing of particular experiences in relationship — the poet, not yet the philosopher; words that are rooted in images of the living and in personal experience, rather than in the search for universal meanings conditioned by social experience (Sagittarius).

In Sagittarius the Night-force operates with great intensity, and, as always, it manifests as a tendency to gather-in many and distant factors through *generalization*. But, with the Day-force so vitally active in Gemini, the basic trend is one toward *particularization and personalization*. Thus, the process of "vivid extension" which Gemini represents deals with extension in terms of particulars, of concrete experience; and the aim of this extension is the building of a personality and of a basis for the operation of personality: the home (Cancer).

At more complex levels of mental development, we find the Gemini force manifesting as a craving for classification, for ordered enumeration, for logic; that is for structural patterns of association. The individual filled with the energy of the Day-force tends to be overwhelmed by the complexity of his personal experience. There is so much that is felt, touched, dimly sensed. The world is so full of flowers, the nights so sparkling, the fire of self flames forth in such intricate designs of living that some definite order must be evolved at any cost if the budding personality is not to be shattered by the very vividness of this "extension of being."

Thus, Gemini must classify, must force into set categories the multiplicity of the things sensed, must produce words to help memorize the fragrance of fleeting experiences, must impose logical moulds upon the elusiveness of human contacts. It needs to find guiding lines of reference, a framework for its activities. Conveniently it discovers polar opposites, good and evil, right and wrong as compass-points by which to steer its course. It symbolizes personal feelings into cosmic entities. Exteriorize it must. And behold! The world is being peopled with gods and elementals, with demons and "Masters." Words they are; projections of experiences duly classified and to which names have been given — names which serve as screens to guard the immature personality from the shock of unexpected experiences and metamorphoses; names which are useful means to make one feel securely on familiar ground; props for the living.

This search for personal, intellectual security in the midst of ever-changing flow of experiences gave birth to Greek logic, to the syllogism, to classical European science as conceived by Descartes. As man began to develop more autonomous and less instinctual forms of thinking, he found himself in an unfamiliar realm of psychological complexities and of mental transformations swift as lightning. Who could hold the evanescent thoughts? Who was not afraid of the strange pranks of the mind, of that mind whose dangerous uncertainties made it be called "the slayer of the Real"?

Logic was built — as "good and evil" were built — to give men more security in the midst of the bewildering flow of experiences summoned by the Day-force and its ever-shifting eagerness for new things, new sensations, new feelings, new thrills, new dreams. They were built, first, for the individuals who pioneered into the newly opened realms of personal psychological experience; realms soon to be filled with safeguards and *taboos* for the unwary or for the weak. Gods and syllogisms, masters and algebras have been, and still are, necessary protections for men who are so insecure in their own individual identity, so close to the racial-biological womb of collective instincts, so easily swayed by the fumes of blood that the danger of "breakdown of personality" is always lurking in the shadowy darkness of the psyche.

Particular systems and set techniques originate in such a need which gave birth, as well, to all mythologies. The birth of full and free individual Personality is such a momentous happening in the evolutionary process of the universe that every phase of it must be prepared carefully. Words are safety devices; they reduce the unfamiliar to collective normality. Ethical systems and logic set limits beyond which catastrophe to the too daring person looms as a constant menace. All such structures are only fully developed as social factors during the Sagittarius phase of the cycle, but in Gemini the individual *must* originally create them. He creates them out of his vital personal need, with all the vividness of an imagination stirred by new relationships which can only be faced and related to past experiences if they are given names; he creates them as a poet. And originally every poet is a "Magician."

Gemini man is the bestower of names, thus the magician who can control nature-forces by uttering their "true names." Words of power, incantations, magical formulas are the earliest forms of poetry; and, in time, all culture flows from this first attempt at meeting with assurance and positive will the unfamiliar and the mysterious entities of the night. In Gemini, man feels already the incoming surge of the Night-force. He knows he must face it. He prepares to build for himself a home to meet the stranger — who is also the Beloved. Personality in its fullness can come out only of such a meeting. And there are such dangerous possibilities to the self in that confrontation that it has to be circumscribed, walled in by more names and more *taboos*: Thus marriage, the home, monogamy and all the social-ethical regulations surrounding this meeting of the self and the other. However, the insecurity which Gemini feels is different in quality from that of the Aries period. It is not a vague fear of being drawn back into the past, but the very concrete realization that set structures and formulations *must* be built if what is being experienced is not to be utterly lost or is not to scatter the personality into a multiplicity of incoherent reactions to ever-new experiences.

A full understanding of what is implied in the activity of the human person during the Gemini phase of his experience should rest on the recognition of two basic types of organic relationships. It is because, during that phase, there is for every man the possibility of transferring the center of his consciousness from one type to the other that the psychological problems particular to Gemini arise.

The first type of relationship belongs to the realm of Taurus. It is *earth-relationship*, symbolized by the fact that every plant that grows on the surface of our planet is rooted in the same soil. As there is only one continuous crust of the earth (continuous even under the oceans) all plants are related to one another by their roots. The fir tree in the Rocky Mountains, the pine in Georgia and the oak in the European mountains all emerge from the same solid and compact earth-surface. Such a type of connection characterizes essentially all relationships which come under the Sign Taurus: relationship through the "roots" of the being (physical contact, food, sex, etc.) — relationship defined by a common bondage to the earth, and in general to the factor of "fruitful substance" at any conceivable level.

The other kind of unifying relationship is *relationship through the air*; the air which all living organisms breathe — be they plants, animals or human beings. We are all, actually and in concrete fact, united with every breathing organism. However separate and proud we may be in our feeling of superiority and decency as we walk along Park Avenue, we take willy nilly in the innermost depths of our being (lungs and blood) the very same air which a moment ago has been breathed by a very dirty peddler, a prostitute or a criminal in the slums nearby. We might not ever think of being in the same room with these people, but the air they have breathed is now in our lungs. We cannot escape the relationship; for to do so would mean swift death. The narrow circle of our conscious relationships to other human beings is thus *extended*, against our will, by the air we breathe.

Air likewise unites us in our basic mode of expression, speech; for sound travels by means of air-waves. Air-waves relate us in our home to the airplane soaring a mile above, as we hear the sound of the engine. Air carries the pollen which gives us hay fever. However thick the walls of the fortified castle we build around our precious ego, however proud or selfish our "isolationism" — air laughs at these childish fancies of ours and compels us to be related, to be one with the very things we wish to escape. Air is therefore truly the element through which man may experience a basic "extension of relationships." And Gemini is known as the first of the "air signs" of the Zodiac.

A vivid extension of being through the constant search for ever new relationships: this is the essence of human experience in Gemini. This extension began at the biological level when the human hand emerged as a new evolutionary factor in the realm of living organisms. Indeed, the hand — "ruled" by Gemini — is the primordial symbol of the human kingdom at the level of organic life. Through the use of the hand, man became a maker of tools. The variety of his experiences increased enormously as these tools enabled him to control and change his environment. New associations led to new patterns of relationship and to the progressive refinement of nervous reactions and nervous sensitiveness. From hands to nerves and to brains: this is a Gemini-controlled process of personality development. Along its course, man, the thinker — progeny of man, the maker — is born.

In Aries, man does not experience thinking as an associative process based on the raw materials of his personal experience. He experiences "ideas" — which strike him from above, or germinate within him as seeds from the past, seeds which belong to the phase of the previous cycle when the Night-force was dominant. Through Taurus, these ideas or inspirational revelations of meaning sink themselves into the substance of human feelings and organic reactions. Only in Gemini does thought really occur as a consistent and functional process of organic behavior under the direction of the Day-force.

Thinking controlled by the energy of the Day-force is quite a different thing from thinking dominated, in Sagittarius, by the Night-force. Gemini thinking is, on one hand, related to the needs of the personality, and on the other, it is something absorbed from the environment. It is *learnt*. At whatever level it might be, Gemini thinking is transmitted thinking; thinking which brings into concrete expression the impulses and inspirations experienced during the Aries period. It is verbal thinking conditioned by language. The Gemini thinker selects from the treasure-house of past civilization's words and concepts as means for him to grow as a personality. He thinks *psychologically*; whereas the typical Sagittarian thinks *socially*. And this is why Gemini is poet rather than philosopher. He builds with words, as the hands build with clay, stones and wood. But he builds because he personally *must* grow through that experience, because in that building, he trains himself to function as an autonomous and consistent personality.

...College years; years of apprenticeship, of wanderings into new worlds, of being drawn and repelled by touch and smiles, deeply uncertain yet aggressively sure, the more set the less the flow of life seems seizable by hands and brains, projecting symbols, images, words to reassure oneself that one is knower and master — such is the Gemini phase: the entrance into the wide world of human society, the gates to the great experience of union with the Beloved.

CANCER

With the summer solstice, a climactic point in the year's cycle is reached. The longest day meets the shortest night, the triumphant Day-force streaming forth from the noon-day Sun begins to wane before the ascendant power of the Night-force. Summer has come and the glory of fruitions. But fruition and fulfillment create new realizations and new tasks. Out of "union" is born the duty to direct the process of formation, and of growth, of the results of that union; and, first of all, the need to circumscribe expansion in order to bring these forces of formation and growth *to the clearest possible focus.*

The Zodiacal Sign Cancer represents the principle of focalization of formative life-energies for the purpose of producing as clear-cut and as permanent an image or impression as possible. It therefore brings a reversal of trend to the process of vivid extension of being through new relationships which Gemini started. Just as Taurus repolarizes the direction of the Day-force in Aries, so Cancer redirects the energies of Gemini. Taurus and Cancer are considered as "feminine" Signs. Taurus' "earth" is needed to arrest and to complete the "fire" of Aries. Cancer's "water" condenses the "airy" extension and the all-penetrating quality of Gemini.

Gemini spreads its search for new relationships over the whole world of experience; even as it builds words, sentences and intellectual systems, it does so with a peculiar abandon and lack of concern for ultimate results. All that the Gemini person seeks to achieve is personal security in making ever-new contacts. He seeks temporary intellectual control through verbal formulation. He takes care that in extending himself he remains always within familiar structures. Therefore, he never discards his own spectacles, but he carries these spectacles to every land and situation possible. He would not care if anyone else used or did not use such spectacles, except that being well-known as the originator of a particularly good kind of spectacles makes it easier for him to establish advantageously many more new contacts.

For instance, in matters of love Gemini will take care to have his approach to the opposite sex well defined in his own mind, so that the shock of being overwhelmed by a love of elemental power may be avoided. He will classify his reactions, his types of women, while pushing always forward and to new horizons his curiosity and eagerness for love. And if he likes to be known as a Don Juan it is only because such a reputation may "extend more vividly" the field of his contacts. Gemini may become completely bound by his formulations and categories, by his logic and his expectations; but he is only *personally* bound. He does not insist that other people should be likewise bound by the same patterns; thus, he can be tolerant, and he loves fair play, yet he is at the same time quite unable to get actually the other person's point of view.

He has tolerance but no real understanding; whereas Sagittarius can have understanding even when he is most intolerant, for Sagittarius can perceive sympathetically how a social situation produced in a person a certain attitude, and he may not blame the person. But if he does not approve of the situation and attitude, he will probably act with extreme intolerance with regard to the *ideas* implied — even though he may understand and sympathize with the *person* holding the ideas.

In Cancer we witness a sudden cancellation of Gemini's eager extension. Boundaries are reached; the curiosity for new relationships is absorbed by an event which leads to a complete reversal of motion. The Sun stops in northern skies, and sunsets begin to bend southward. There is a brief pause, and all things change polarity. The Day-force has reached its maximum intensity. It must slowly let itself be superseded by the matriarchal power of the Night-force. Wherever extension had reached, there definite boundaries are set. If they are to be pushed back still farther, it will be on a new basis of activity; on a social and mental, rather than on a physiological and personal, basis.

What has really happened to affect the reversal? Just this, that the individual self, being no longer able to resist the pressure of the universal life-force, has had to open itself to the universe and to society. Such an opening up could theoretically occur in any way best fitted to the individual's need. And it does occur freely and at every moment in the man who has reached a certain level of integration and freedom; in the man who has become free from the results of frustration and repressions imposed upon his growth by parents and antecedents, by the past of his race — and if one believes in reincarnation — of his Soul; free from subconscious as well as conscious memories.

But in the ordinary man of today such memories, frustrations and failures are strong. Subconscious fears have arisen in Aries, biological-racial inertia and possessiveness in Taurus, intellectually crystallized formulations in Gemini. Thus, when the individual faces, in Cancer, the reversal of his life-force and is flooded by universal life or confronted with the need of participating in human society after he has "come of age," the confrontation is highly upsetting. Irrational, biological, emotional, devotional forces rush from the unconscious and tend to overwhelm the conscious. Therefore, the individual must be protected; the onsurge of the unconscious must be canalized, made safer. And this need is the reason for "marriage" and for what the occultist calls "Initiation." One mate and one Initiator — whereas all life could be mate and Initiator, if men had the integrative strength sufficient not to be overwhelmed by the ever-changing confrontations life would present to him; if man were conscious enough to be at any time and in any condition a focal point for universal life — for God. And he would have no need of a wife or of child-bearing to force upon him in a particular way — and in only one such manner — the realization that his goal and his fulfillment are to be found in the discharge of his *responsibility to life*, in his conscious willingness to be a focus in and through which Life or God may speak.

God might speak through the individual in myriads of voices, one for the need of every moment. But because the individual grew under the malformative influence of fear, inertia and mental crystallization, the stone of man is not a clear crystal. It must be ground. The individual must love and suffer, bend to homely tasks and deprivation, yearn amidst brief happiness and "give up his self" to find "Life eternal." Yet fulfillment, in essence and reality, is here and now. There is nothing to "give up," but fallacies. All that is needed to become a lens able to focus divinity is to become consciously what one inherently *is*, and to be it with clarity, in beauty and in truth.

A lens to focus life. For the ordinary man at this stage of human evolution life here means "humanity"; it could mean, it will mean someday "divinity." The home and the "human, all too human" marriage are conditioned by the factor of "humanity" and "society," by the education received by the child, by parental frustrations. Abnormal development in childhood and adolescence makes the youth cling to the Day-force; makes him want it to grow and grow through an ever-extended Gemini phase. He should willingly and understandingly open himself to the increase of the Night-force. Such is the lesson of the summer solstice, of Cancer. There must be repolarization; but humanity today must be *compelled* to repolarize itself. It must be compelled to open itself to the Night-force, the Mystery of Space and the Brotherhood of the Stars; for it would not do it willingly, whether as individuals or as nations. And this is our present world problem.

What is the nature of that compulsion? A sudden arousal of the irrational, instinctual, biological forces rooted in the blood; a sudden arousal of "feelings," of psychic visions also. We call this, "falling in love"; today also, in the social sphere, we call it mass-devotion to dictators extolling the "call of the blood" — or to Prophets who bring to men in one particular form (whence dogmatism) the Revelation from God. These are various aspects of the same process in the individual and in humanity: this process is the change from Gemini to Cancer, that "conversion" which reverses the direction of the life-force.

Let us realize that it need not be a violent, fanatic, passionate "conversion." The biological-emotional or religious urge need not overwhelm the consciousness; but it *will* overwhelm it of necessity where the consciousness is un-free, set in ego crystallizations, unyielding, or steeped in "complexes" and glamour. That means, alas! mostly everywhere. And thus, we have organized and set totalitarianism in all realms — enforced unity — as a perhaps unavoidable safeguard against utter disintegration; moral disintegration in the individual, anarchy in human society.

So few persons have understood the mystery of the symbol of Cancer, the Crab! A watery creature, whose movements are regressive or side-stepping, whose evolution has been led into the blind alley constituted by the wearing of a hard shell encasing life — yet a shell which is temporarily shed at every new cycle, one must not forget! A creature of the *sea*; and the sea always symbolizes the collective or rather, the *generic,* Unconscious, the universal Matrix of life.

Here we have just as negative a type of symbolization as we find in Scorpio. One step further and we find the connection between Cancer and the deadly disease of the same name. Why such a negative emphasis? Because the Ancients who built this zodiacal symbolism knew well that the real, positive, God-releasing significance of the summer solstice could hardly be given out. In the Western world we have to go to Christian scriptures to find more complete references to the summer solstice as to the "Marriage of Heaven and Earth"; of Christ and the Bride, humanity: Christ focused through the mystic Incarnation in man. But in India, if we only understand the real meaning of the concept of *Avatar*, of ideas which presumably the great Shankaracharya taught — he who was born with the Sun in Cancer — then we would grasp the real significance of this birth of the summer. This might help us to understand our own United States and our potential world-destiny, as we too were born nationally under the Sign, Cancer. Is it not significant indeed that our most dreaded disease today has also been named cancer?

Is the higher destiny of the Cancer type to build a particular, set and rigid home, or is it rather to serve as a focus for a new manifestation of God? Is the United States fulfilled in a narrow nationalism, in homes so badly broken up by crystallized complex-ridden individualism and consequent divorces; or is our world-destiny that of being — at a time when many nations have "fallen in love" with dictators and blood-rooted, home-extolling totalitarianism — a focal point for a new, world encompassing Avatar-force? Cancer comes nine months before the future Aries. Cancer is the symbol of fecundation — but will it be a divine or a strictly human fecundation? Cancer is man in the God-impregnated state; a Holy Place in which God has descended.

In the usual practice of astrology, the type of personality characterized by Cancer is represented as being often dominated by moods and psychic gifts. What is not always realized is that these psychic manifestations are the results of an irruption of the universal life-force into the individualized consciousness which becomes more or less disorganized thereby. Such an irruption can mean a great many things; from the peculiar rapture of passionate love to the upsets of the first weeks of pregnancy, from psychic hallucinations to God-inspired seership, from glamorous lies to Avatarship. And we must not forget the recoil from this irruption of the Night-force, the clinging to a particular form, a particular home, a particular feeling, the jealousies and possessiveness which are the shadows of the integration of one man and one woman — all born of fear, of the terrific fear of what might happen with a "change of focus."

The Cancer type contains all that. It can be the most helpless or the most determined in a strange, silent way. It refers to a time of the year when the Sun moves very slowly; stands still. There is a stillness about it at the same time that there is the possibility of intense light. It is the moment of the longest days; yet astrology makes it ruled by the Moon, waiting until one more sign to glorify in Leo the creative radiance of the Sun.

This is because all great sacraments come when there is a pause, silence and tremor. Man possessed by God, or by the Beloved, is at first overwhelmed by the union. Everything must be reconsidered, all motion and motives reversed. And in those short intense nights, when the Feast of St. John is celebrated, there may be tumult in the outer world, but there is stillness in the Holy Place where Night enfolds Day, and Life is conceived anew.

LEO

Throughout the stage of human experience represented by Cancer two basic needs are impressed upon the evolving personality. One of them is the need for a clear-cut focusing — and thus limiting — of the energies of the Day-force whose strength had become overwhelming; the other is the need to assume responsibility toward one's fellow men and to participate consciously in the life of a social whole.

While the Day-force can be defined as a "personalizing energy," forcing into concrete and particular actuality abstract patterns, ideas or spiritual entities, the Night-force is an "in-gathering energy" bringing personalities together in the process of building social groups. The foundation of that social process is — at least in our present phase of human development — the home and family. Cancer is the symbol of that foundation, the well-spring of the Night-force which will wax in strength and influence until the winter solstice is reached with Capricorn (the symbol of completely organized social living: the all-powerful State).

The zodiacal Sign Leo represents the second phase of that social process. In Leo, the power that compelled the individual man and woman to limit, stabilize and deepen each other within the social root-pattern of a home, is now urging them to create a progeny. Thus, they are made to assume a new social responsibility. A new field of integration is opened up: the integration of parents to children, of older to younger generations. Out of this, truly *social* issues will arise; problems of relationship which cannot easily be broken because they involve the responsibility of the "present" (which is constantly becoming the "past") to the "future." Thus, time begins to lay its weight upon the individual's consciousness.

Time is a very powerful factor in all creative activity and all social relationships. We might say that time means very little in normal adolescence; that it is lost in the glamour of love during the honeymoon. But when the child (and all creative activities) brings to the parents a new burden of responsibility, then time begins to be an actual, often poignant reality. The mother knows it for the first time with the depth of her being through her nine-month pregnancy. The father experiences it through the discipline of a "schedule of work" in the life of social activity and responsibility which then begins to confront him. He experiences it as a father at home, and as an executive or manager in the sphere of his work, even if he "manages" only his own tasks.

When we wrote "for the first time" and "begins to experience" we were obviously referring to conditions of living such as prevailed in archaic societies based on the normal rhythm of biological growth; societies such as, for instance, prevailed in the India of old. Modern societies, on the other hand, are transitional affairs, chaotic, non-organized; and thus, the normal biological-psychological rhythm of human development, which the Zodiac accurately symbolizes, no longer operates with clarity or precision. Yet the Zodiac remains a potent symbol of a natural process which some day will again serve as a basis for the organization of society and even of personality. It will be a kind of organization encompassing much more than the old civilizations did include, an organization at several levels of human activity; but it will be organization just the same, and along natural lines made visible by the symbolic pageant of Sun, Moon and stars.

Leo is the realm of emotions, in contradistinction to Cancer which is that of "feelings." These two terms, feelings and emotions, should be clearly distinguished from one another. "Feeling" is an internal and organic sense, by means of which the personality as a whole (or at the strictly biological level, the body as a whole) passes judgment on what is constructive and destructive, good and bad for the entire human being. To "feel" is to react as an organic whole to a situation and a person — and reacting thus means simply reacting for or against the situation or entity confronting the person who feels.

As a result of, or synchronously with, such a "feeling" a number of things happen. Muscles contract. The blood pressure is raised or lowered, the pulse accelerated or delayed, however imperceptibly it may be. The endocrine glands also react to that "feeling," secreting more or less of their products in the blood. Organic chemistry is thus ever so slightly altered. All these *organic changes* constitute, psychologically speaking, the "affect" or emotion; and the emotion either transforms itself into an action (kissing or running away, for instance), or else is stopped from manifesting outwardly into a *visible* muscular action. Emotions, therefore, follow feelings: but the two must be clearly differentiated. The feelings belong to the realm of the Sign Cancer; emotions, to that of Leo.

There are also what may be called "internal feelings." A man feels well or feels sick. Such feelings are the direct manifestations of the way in which the organism as a whole operates. The moment one of the functions of the organism is impaired or inhibited, the human being feels that there is something wrong. In a localized and acute sense, the feeling of organic disturbance is "pain." Through external and internal feeling, and above all through pain, man gains progressively a sense of being a separate unit, somehow different from other similar organisms. Man learns to say "I." He learns to say it at first through pain and frustration; that is, by not having what his organism needs or desires. He learns to operate as a "personal ego," different from other personal egos because he "feels" in a different way. Individualization begins through pain and the exercise of feelings. It grows through man's attempts at self-expression (the realm of Leo). It becomes set through the exercise of the power of intellectual analysis and discrimination (the realm of Virgo).

In Cancer the human being becomes: at the *biological* level, an organism with a definite lifespan and rhythm of growth; at the *psychological* level, a person — an organism of feelings centered around an ego; at the *social* level, the owner of a home which defines his social status. At each level what is built in Cancer is the basic capacity to meet, as an integrated whole (an organism), the impact of other entities, and to establish a foundation from which one may be able to operate creatively and socially. In Leo, man goes forth from this foundation and, with a still somewhat insecure determination to be a "social" person, he "moves-out" into the world brandishing his "yes" and his "no" as a flashing sword. In Cancer, the human person is like a square or cube — a foundation. In Leo, he is an ego straining his — to him — glorious "I am" as a standard which will lead to victory.

Leo has been often interpreted as the most individualistic sign of the Zodiac; but it is so only if one defines the term "individualistic" in relation to social relationships and everyday life in groups. In Leo the individual, having begun to feel a responsibility to beloved and child, is impelled to participate in some kind of social activity; no longer as an adolescent in school, but as an independent personality having to determine his course of action and to be responsible for his failures. The result of such a situation is that the personality, at the Leo stage of experience, *overdoes* everything. He wants to make an impression upon society, very much as a seven-year-old child wants to make a big impression on his intimates. He feels that he is "the thing"; that of course everyone will see at once how important he will be to society, and that quickly they will bow to his unusual abilities and bestow upon him riches and power — riches and power he needs not only to feed, but even more to lord it over, his wife and children.

Thus, the keynote of Leo is: *dramatic exteriorization of personality in order to gain social recognition and increased self-assurance as a social unit.* The Leo type may not necessarily be a leader by right of ability. But, if so, he will undoubtedly attempt, even if in small ways, to bluff or push his way through, with big theatrical gestures, emotional fireworks and much gambling — for Leo likes to take risks as much as to manage people. But just as the so-called "aggressiveness" of the Aries type is the result of his sense of *personal* insecurity, so the dramatic bids for leadership and the generosity of the Leo type is a psychological compensation for an often poignant — withal unacknowledged and most likely unconsciousness of — *social* insecurity.

Mussolini, whose youthful photographs betray his early sense of social inferiority and his neurotic character, is an excellent example of the course a true Leo type will or may pursue. If he finds himself in the midst of confused and disheartened people he will at once sense his chance and rise to the occasion; power will build him up in an amazing way and he will glow just as an adulated "young prodigy" usually does — and likewise he may collapse into obscurity when the tide of success turns and the Virgo phase of self-criticism and self-mortification begins to operate. Then the proud Leo may astonish everyone by big public gestures of self-humiliation. He takes all the blame. There is no more convincing penitent. But he may soon forget and begin another cycle of social self-aggrandizement.

Such a reliance on social gestures and gambles is a sure sign that, fundamentally, the man is not sure; often that he is actually filled with social fears. He does not know how to cooperate with people; so he has to lead them. Leadership in the manner of dictators means projecting oneself forcefully upon receptive materials. The creative artist acts likewise. Whatever be his field of creation, he encounters resistance from the materials upon which he projects his vision and his emotional intensity; but that resistance can be overcome by ruthless means. The musical instrument can be forced to resound; the oil can be spread over the canvas if enough insistence is displayed. It is not a matter of cooperating with materials, but of clever handling and of instinctive (or acquired) knowledge of how they react to the touch. Likewise, dictators are adepts in mass-psychology. They use propaganda and they dramatize themselves. And such is the technique of leadership.

True social consciousness is something entirely different. The typical Leo person has very little of it in his make-up; even though he may give the impression he has. He speaks in terms of generalities. He stirs crowds with words and dreams. He hypnotizes people through the intensity of his self-projection. But his wife often knows better; for dramatic gestures need foot-lights and distance to be really effective.

Nevertheless, there is something fascinating and compelling about a true Leo type showering upon large groups his solar radiance. One may be overwhelmed, as by the glare and heat of summer noons; yet, if one can find a tree in the shade of which to rest, it is a beautiful spectacle. The sun, indeed, is the great Autocrat of the solar system. Is it because he is rather a small star — some occult books even say "a lost star"? Nevertheless, to all that are drawn within his orb of radiation he gives generously of self and of life; though he also may kill and produce wastes, unless clouds and rains intervene to mother those whom the great Autocrat would glorify — to death.

In the Leo phase of the zodiacal cycle the Day-force is waning; but while it is waning in terms of effective manifestation, nevertheless this decrease means as well an inward withdrawal and subconscious activity. The Day-force has begun to move inward into man's subconscious; just as the Night-force had done during winter and spring. It still operates; but in a subjective and introverted manner. It takes on transcendent characteristics — and in some cases, negative ones.

Personality, which had been fulfilled in its physical and natural aspect at the summer solstice and throughout Cancer, acquires in Leo, as it were, a new dimension. Art is born, often a refuge for sensitive natures and an escape from everyday social realities; but also, a transcendental and symbolic projection of the normally focused and integrated personality. The man who cannot be an autocrat — or, following a modification of that urge to power, the teacher of children and receptive adults — can gain social usefulness and prestige through artistic activity. In such a type of activity we find combined an unyielding individualism, the urge to be alone and self-concentrated, and the need to impress oneself upon society.

Creative artistic expression, in as much as it uses socially accepted and traditional materials, and in proportion as it commands fame and perhaps financial support, is a socially conditioned activity. Yet it is also a means of extending one's personal selfhood inward and *beyond the limitations of time*. It is a means to reach personal immortality through a fame perpetuated from generation to generation; thus, to negate or overcome time. And it is also a method for expanding one's own consciousness; for teaching oneself.

The artist, at his best, performs a kind of *yoga* while creating. He is not only intensely concentrated, but the symbols he paints or the energies he rouses through tones are often real messages from his deeper Identity. In creation, the outer self (being concentrated and devoted to the task) becomes a receptive surface; just as receptive and expectant as the canvas or the piano. Therefore, it can be moulded by what pours from within; by the Teacher within, the Inner Ruler.

The main negative manifestation of the inwardly operating Day-force in Leo is an extreme of sensitiveness to anything that seems to challenge personal dignity and pride. The Day-force is waning; thus, it is no longer building directly the personality. Personality expands still, but on a social basis; that is, in terms of social approval and support. Anything which tends to lessen this social sustainment seems therefore to challenge the very right of the personality to live, and causes great resentment or hurt. Thus, the extreme sensibility of artists and dictators to criticism or loss of public favor. Thus, the Leo type's willingness, in many cases, to use any means to maintain or regain such a favor; including dramatic over-statements, lies and bribery.

Leo is the individual in his first attempt to be a social personage. And, as with any first effort, he often fails; or, for fear of failing, he overdoes and over-dramatizes situations. He has yet to learn not to want to be a master of subordinates, because of his being absolutely sure he can never become a subordinate. Indeed, he is instinctively fighting against his subconscious fears that society might absorb and enslave him. Thus, his exaggerated attitudes and the intensity of his projections. And because he senses acutely the power of the universe and of time over his socially un-adjusted ego, he must create; and he stamps his own ego upon the world which he wills to organize in his own likeness, so that he be not lost in the onsurging tide.

VIRGO

In Virgo, the evolving consciousness of man is mainly occupied with analyzing, reacting against or developing further all that occurred during the Leo period. In Leo, we saw a type of adjustment in which the Night-force, as yet hesitant and un-sure in its social adjustments, often compels the individual to over-stress his own emotional projections. Having found a foundation in his home and "taken root," the individual is confronted with social responsibilities. He must participate in society on the basis of his home and his personal independence. He came of age symbolically at the summer solstice. Now he must play his part in society. He must produce, beget, create. He is poignantly aware — even if not clearly conscious — of that "must." He pushes himself. He assumes the responsibility of management. He sets policies. He is full of himself, radiant in his fatherhood — but he is not accustomed, as yet, to act in terms of social responsibility. His adventuring often leads to failure; his cocksureness, to blundering. He is hurt; his pride, wounded. He has given out so much that his body feels the wear and tear of overwork, over-emotionalism — perhaps of excesses of all sorts.

If the Leo-type is a mother, childbearing and its consequent tasks may have led to bodily strain and psychic weariness. Thus, the discharge of home and social responsibilities may have left very deep marks. Procreation and creative activity, work and excessive enjoyment may have posited serious problems. In short, all is not well. What can be done about it? Questions without end arise in the confused mind. Who can give adequate answers? One must go on working, producing, teaching, investing, creating. That is the very essence of social living. But how can one go on with strength and faith vanishing? Who can teach the technique of activity in ease, of work without strain?

At this stage, the Virgo phase of the unfoldment of consciousness begins. It begins with a question mark. It *may* end with true Illumination at the fall equinox, as Libra begins. It should end with a greater understanding of the meaning of the social process, of the nature of the Night-force. It should end in beauty and peace, or at least in social adjustment.

Productive activity on the basis of strict individualism and emotional self-expression presents to man a riddle. How can physical and nervous exhaustion, emotional tragedy and disillusionment be avoided? In essence, this is the question which man everlastingly asks of the Sphinx; and there is a fitting tradition which says that the point of the Zodiac which ends the sign Leo and begins the sign Virgo carries the symbol of the Sphinx. This mythical creature, which still faces today the sands of Egypt, has the body of a lion and the head of a virgin — this is indeed the meeting point of Leo and Virgo. It symbolizes the answer to the eternal query which we have just stated. What is this answer?

The answer is two-fold; yet the two sides of it should be integrated and that integration, difficult in practice though simple in theory, is the very secret of the Sphinx, which is two beings in one. One side of the answer refers to the wear and tear produced by the impulsive and stressful type of activity and its dramatic gestures. The answer can be summed up in one word: *Technique*. The other side of the picture deals with a *repolarization* of the emotional nature itself. Technique and emotional repolarization are the two keys to the secret of the Sphinx.

A technique is a method based on fundamental principles, the application of which enables a man to perform his work with ease, with a minimum of wear and tear, waste or destructive strain, and in the shortest time possible. The worker who understands thoroughly the foundation of the method and has built its mode of application in the very structure of his muscular, nervous and mental behavior — is a master of technique.

Technique must be learned. Barring very unusual cases, it must be learned from one who is a "master of technique." Thus, he who wants to learn the secret of smooth, easy and supremely effective performance has to become an *apprentice*. He must become objective to his own ways of behavior. He must analyze them and refuse to be blind to their defects. He must be absolutely honest and un-glamoured in the evaluation of any performance: his and others' also. He must learn to criticize dispassionately and without prejudice. He must be keen in discrimination. He must be "pure."

Purity is a much misunderstood term, loaded usually with confusing ethical and traditional images. For water to be "pure water" means to be water without any sediment, dirt or organic substances such as microbes and the like. It is to be *nothing but* what the chemist describes by the formula H_2O. Likewise, for a man to be "pure" is to be "nothing but" what he is inherently and by the right of his own individual destiny.

When a man contains in his nature elements and desires which "do not belong" to the pattern of his essential individual character and destiny, these factors act as "impurities"; and they cause psychological conflicts and breakdowns. If there are particles of dirt or water in gasoline, the performance of the car's engine is uneven and hectic. It causes wear and tear in the engine. Likewise, a man usually collects throughout his childhood and his school-days all kinds of "dirt" or substances foreign to his true individual nature. The alloy of his character contains impurities which will destroy the smoothness of his life-performance. Complexes, born of youthful frustrations and resentments or fears, act as water in the gasoline. They lessen his usable energy. They disrupt the delicate adjustment of his psychological and mental "carburetor." He gets it "out of tune" and his forces are wasted in useless strain and in unproductive expenditure of energy.

Technique means a method to eliminate all impurities which lead to waste of power; to make of the worker a "pure" agent of production, without conflicts, complexes or fears. A master-technician is absolutely sure of himself, because he knows that within himself there is nothing to inhibit, confuse or disturb his performance — nothing in his physical and psychological mechanisms, nothing in the flow of his power from source to point of effective distribution. His hands are sure because his nerves are steady; and his nerves are steady because his psychological nature is clear and unencumbered with waste products or crystallizations born originally of fear.

Technique is thus based on "purity." It also depends on potency and skill. Potency means that the performer has been born with unimpaired organs of action through which the universal life-force can flow in a condition of relatively high potential; it means, even more, that such life-potential has not been *used up*. Thus, the symbolism of the "Virgin" — who is "pure" and "potent," because unpolluted and filled with unused energies.

Skill, born of adequate training, comes last. In a sense, training would not be so necessary, or at least the length of it could be considerably reduced, if the apprentice were really pure and potent; because the life-force, flowing then at maximum intensity and without corruption, would have the *ability to adjust itself rapidly to any new situation.* Unfortunately, men today forget that fact. They put all the stress upon mechanical training; whereas, if all personal obstacles were removed and the individual had real potency, the most complicated mechanism could be mastered with a very small amount of practical experience. Life *is* intelligence. Men have obstructed that inherent intelligence by social and personal fallacies; thus, they have to substitute tedious training for it. But give life a real chance, through a couple or more generations, and miracles could happen.

This is obviously not meant to lessen the value of training, but only to show that at least half of the apprentice's task is to clear himself from hindrances; the rest is relatively easy. Thus, *self-purification* is the essential means to technical mastery. Man must become again a "virgin." The past must be forgotten, eradicated — remaining only as an "essence of experience" giving depth to consciousness, but not affecting the structures of mind, emotions and body with crystallized memories which always mean blockages, thus waste and ineffectiveness. *Self-revitalization* ensues — the re-opening of the deep well whence power may once more flow through renewed channels of release. Then *familiarity with new devices*, from which skill will almost automatically follow. True skill, however, is not based on habits and memorized rules, but on the ability to adjust oneself immediately to any and all situations and to the requirements of any and all mechanisms.

All of the preceding analysis deals with the factor of technique; and the student of astrology will have easily recognized in these statements the several characteristics which astrological text books attribute on the basis of traditional authority to the zodiacal sign Virgo:

analysis, discrimination, criticism, routine of work, purity, self-integrity, care of the body, hygiene, training, etc. But Virgo offers also another answer to the seeker after self-perfection; to the thwarted, bruised and embittered soul who after rushing, in Leo, after emotional self-expression finds itself empty and broken-hearted; also, to the parents whose progeny turned ungrateful, to the creative artist whose creations aroused no social response, to the leaders whose following deserted him.

That answer of the Sphinx is: *emotional repolarization.* "What caused your emotional disillusionment and bitterness?" — asks the Sphinx. And, looking into the hollowed eyes of the stone-image which turn into mirrors reflecting our innermost depths, we realize at last that our emotional failures have been due mostly to our lack of "social sense." We have ignored the meaning of the Night-force, of that cosmic power which gathers-in all units into greater organisms and dispassionately, un-emotionally establishes complex patterns of relationship into which everything may fit. We have insisted that our way of projecting our emotions was the only way; that we had the right to demand everything or nothing, the right to force our conditions upon life. And the Night-force turned destructive; we became lost in the dark and frightened by the broken echoes of our own desires.

"Look at me," says the Sphinx, "become like unto me. My lion-like passions are strong. I am a huge feline in whose groins ardent power lies. But my head is that of a virgin. I am still, waiting for that which must come. I behold the stars. I wait for my time, which is written. In me, there is no pride and no haste. In me, power and purity are polarized toward the fulfillment of purpose and destiny."

The Night-force is the power of more-than-individual purpose. It is the womb of greater selfhood, of vaster life-organizations. It gathers-in the small selves in expectation of the Greater Self, which will come at the appointed time. The message of Virgo to the sufferers is therefore: "Look beyond yourself. Reorganize your desires, re-polarize your emotions, reorient your impulses. Your energies are not yours; they are life's. You hold them in trust for humanity as a whole. Be sure they serve a purpose greater than your littleness, greater even than home and family. Consecrate them to the Greater Whole."

Virgo is thus, in one of its aspects, the realm of devotion and spiritual discipleship. It is the realm of the individual's subservience to a collective purpose and a collective discipline; the realm of service and self-immolation, of willing sacrifices — as that of the seed becomes bread to feed the hungry one. It is the realm of the Army, because through the discipline and sacrifice of war, man learns forcibly to participate in a Greater Whole: the nation. It is the field of obedience to the structural Law of the universe, of the human species, of the community. In it, man may learn that he who loses his soul finds his divinity. And learning this, he becomes ready to knock at the gates of the Temple; to face the great metamorphosis which awaits him who, having become one with the Sphinx, enters the Pyramid for Initiation.

So much has been written of late about "Initiation"! Yet there is always more to say, because, as in any vital crisis of transformation, everyone facing its challenge and its problems must of necessity go to meet them on the basis of his own relatively unique life-experience. More than this, Initiation means different things to the different parts of the human personality. In terms of technique, it may be represented by the grant of a diploma from the hands of the "University" to which the "master of technique" belonged. In terms of emotional repolarization and of the individual's relationship to a Greater Whole in the life of which he is ready to become a participant, Initiation signifies the end of being alone — if not quite of being lonely.

The lion is king of the desert because he is able, symbolically, to absorb or lord it over all lesser creatures. As he does this, he finds himself alone in the desert. The ego also is alone, because he can only see himself in relation to others as a master of slaves, or as a virtuoso performing for a receptive audience. He is thus alone on the stage, separated from all by the footlights of his pride, of his self-imposed mission — or by the pomp of his regal station. The Virgin is also alone, by definition; but it is a very different kind of aloneness. The Virgin is alone — and expectant. She expects the performance of a Mystery which will destroy both her loneliness and her virginity. She may be afraid of the Unknown. She may stare, Sphinxlike, into the night of the desert; but in her heart and in her womb she *knows* that He will come. That coming will make of the desert a fruitful valley. A people will be born. Libra will come: the communion of men, society, the promise of civilization, the "mystic brotherhood" whose reality is revealed as a concrete fact in the deep chamber of the Pyramid.

When the virgin girl is fecundated by the beloved, it is not only that she mates with one particular man. She opens to human life as a whole. The entire past of the human race floods her expectancy, and she becomes a promise of the future civilization. Likewise, the Collective Unconscious rushes up to the threshold of the conscious in the man who is being "initiated." MAN enters a man. Libra enters Virgo. And Virgo is the expectancy of this advent, the long and arduous preparation for it.

First of all, however, this expectancy is to be aroused. It does not exist in Leo. The Sphinx is the symbolical expression of the crisis which must come at a certain stage of evolution if the creative, self-projective, dramatic aloneness of the human ego (Leo) is to become the expectant, potentially fruitful alone-ness of the human soul (Virgo). This term "soul" is a rather unfortunate one because it has so many different and vague meanings. By it, we mean here the condition of the human psyche — of man's mind and feelings — when it begins to realize that the whole universe does not revolve around itself and that it is a participant in some vast wholeness of being whose seeming infinity is awe-inspiring, yet compelling.

The creative Fire which surges outward in whirling motions from the center of the individualized personality is Leo. Slowly, this Fire becomes aware of Space all around. It faces the cold of Space. It is compelled to slow down its vibratory intensity. Radiant atoms, in ionized states within the Suns, learn to operate as more steady chemical structures. Energy becomes substance. The power in the Lion's loins becomes reason and discrimination in the Virgin's head. Emotional and creative thought-dramas become reflective, analytical understanding. There is a constant process of cooling off. Space overcomes Fire. The Many overcome the One. Relationship triumphs over self-radiation. A sense of the greater Unknown makes all the known glories and all the emotional excitements of the ego-phantasms of questionable value. The expectation of That which would bring this Unknown into the soul is born. It does not matter how this mysterious That is conceived. Already the Lion has become the Virgin: the eternal question mark.

Who is the eternal Unknown who will answer the "Why?" of the Virgin? It is he who, because He has no name, wields the power of Meaning and is the "bestower of names." He is the Initiator whoever answers the riddle of personality and conscious living; He who holds in His mind the secret of the "Measure of Man." But, to find Him, the individual ego must willingly become the neophyte. He must experience training and trial, emotional repolarization and the surrender of his tragic, yet cherished, aloneness. He must welcome the past in understanding, in order that the future may be created in wisdom. He must face the silence in the King's Chamber of the Pyramid — and not be afraid. He must die, and be reborn.

Stillness always descends upon the soul that searches and silently gazes upon distant constellations through the glamorous night of the desert. The Sphinx today still gazes on, though disciples are no longer initiated in the desecrated Pyramid and bombs bring meaningless death to cities nearby. Yet the reality of the Sphinx lives on. Humanity has become the Sphinx. It is asking the eternal question. It is seeking through the global crisis of our days the path to the new Pyramid and the new Initiation — the path to the "Plenitude of Man."

LIBRA

Our symbolical journey along the path of the Zodiac has led us past the awesome countenance of the Sphinx and through the disciplines to be learned during the Virgo period which it opens. Now we face the mysterious structure known to all under the name of the Great Pyramid. Into this structure is stamped the significance of the cosmic reality of the zodiacal Sign, Libra; the significance of the fall equinox and of the ascendancy of the Night-force, victorious over the Day-force. In Libra, Leo's *self-assertion* and Virgo's *self-criticism* are reconciled and overcome through *self-consecration* to Humanity. In this consecration the self remains, but no longer as a master, not even any longer as a critic or a servant. The self remains as a focused lens in and through which the light of the Whole operates, urging all men to become participants in the total organism of Humanity. A participant: a man of action, who works consciously for the triumph of the universal Will over the narrow power of particular egos.

Libra is the birth of the individual unit into the Greater Whole in which he is thenceforth to operate as a cell. The fall equinox marks the decisive triumph of united action and social-cooperation over individualistic self-expression and emotional self-centeredness. It is not yet a final victory; just as the spring equinox does not mean the ultimate phase of personality-building. But, after Libra, the goal ahead should become clear. Vision and understanding are there to be had by every true seeker. New energies are being aroused, energies that are the products of group co-operation and social interchange. New vistas are revealed, new goals more or less clearly outlined. The walls of the fortress of self are — at least theoretically — broken. The life within should be able to combine freely with the life of the companions who eat of the same bread of consecration to the welfare of the Whole; yet who also are ready to fit into a hierarchical pattern of group organization.

The three phases of the process which leads from the fall equinox to the winter solstice parallel rather closely the sequence of development symbolized in the zodiacal Signs, Aries, Taurus and Gemini; but now it is no longer a process of building up of *personality*, but one devoted to the growth of *society*. Socializing forces are surging with ever-increasing momentum. The still scattered individuals are swept by their tide. The entire purpose is that of making more valid, more actual, more tangible the reality of human interchange, the reality of the community, the reality of living together within an organic, stable, permanent structure of communal behavior (Libra). Out of such living together, the energy born of communal feelings and realizations (Scorpio) and the vision born of communal thinking (Sagittarius) will progressively emerge — and finally the completed social organism, the perfected State (Capricorn).

Libra is a cardinal Sign and, thus, in it values of activity or behavior are stressed. The momentum of the social process dynamizes the consciousness of the Libra type. There is great social eagerness, a vital sense of dependence upon social values. This is not the Leo type's dependence upon fame or applause, which was born of unacknowledged social insecurity turning into bravado. The Libra type has developed, for the first time in the zodiacal sequence, a real sense of social value; but just because social values have become so real, so important to that type and because, at the same time, his feelings and emotions are still strongly conditioned by the individualism of the Day-force, the Libra native has a tendency to exaggerate the importance of social factors.

Just as the Aries type becomes aggressive and arrogant in his eagerness to establish himself as an integrated personality, so the Libra type will go out of his way to prove more than is necessary his social sense. He will sacrifice himself — at least he will act as if he did — rather than feel he might be negligent in his social or group obligations. The socializing urge haunts him just as the personalizing urge haunts the Aries type. And yet he is not really sure of himself in social or group activities. He always feels that somehow he could easily revert to individualistic desires; that he has to cover up the possibility of that reversal, to make up for it, to invent stories and stage attitudes to assure his companions — and himself! — that he belongs to the group and the group acts through him.

It has been said that the Libra type is opportunistic, changeful and unreliable. But these are only surface characteristics. The real — because the *psychological* — reason for these Libra traits is that the Libra person is willing to do anything to fit in with what a group or collectivity expects of him; with what *he thinks* the group might expect of him. This makes him changeable and unreliable in surface decisions. It gives him at times the appearance of a chameleon — the symbol of all opportunists — changing his color to fit the situation and, better still, to *merge into situations*. This "merging into situations" is really the essence of the Libra behavior. But underneath *it* there is a very great individual pride and susceptibility, a sometimes harrowing sense of his inability to perform adequately the task he has set for himself — whether in his family or his social life.

Libra and Aries are signs of unstable equilibrium. In them the Day and Night forces are nearly balanced. Thus, the tendency to restlessness, nervousness and often neurotic behavior is often present. In Libra, the person wants *consciously* to be social, impersonal, spiritual, rich in his dealings with his coworkers; yet *subconsciously* he seems, at least to himself, to fall always short of the mark he has set as his ideal goal, and the goal seems ever elusive. Thus, he easily experiences fits of despondency, followed by overzealousness in social work and group-participation. He is ever on the lookout for the ideal group, the ideal form of cooperation. All human relationships seem to him solemn and extremely serious. But he pours himself so intently in them that he may miss the reality by straining himself after the ideal. He may crush the trees in his passionate love for the integrity of the forest.

Yet, at his best, the Libra type is an excellent manager of group activities, a wonderful harmonizer and integrator — the more so perhaps, the more he feels unsure of his own integration. Group-harmony, happiness and idealism in human relationships are matters of life and death for him. Controversies and internal strife upset his nervous balance to the point of complete psychic exhaustion. He has not reached the point where he can thrive on diplomatic intrigues and political schemes, as the Capricorn type does. In Capricorn the social sense is as set and steady as the sense of personality is set in Cancer. But in Libra and Aries, respectively, nothing is yet set. Society and Personality are in the making. Things are just taking shape; so there can hardly be as yet complete ease — just because inadequacy and reversal to past attitudes must appear as appalling tragedies.

Thus, the need for a powerful idealism whenever the Libra type is evolved enough to be really conscious of the social process. Just as the Aries type seeks a Superman or Master upon whom he could lay the insuperable burden of his as yet unsteady personality, so the Libra type pursues his quest for an ideal group or pattern of society to give security to his social endeavors. Thus, the attraction which the Theosophical concept of the "White Lodge" — the perfect group — has had for a number of eager Libra personalities; such as Annie Besant, B. P. Wadia and a few others.[1] Thus, also the high social idealism of one like Gandhi, with his Sun in Libra.

On the other hand, the less evolved type of Libran operates at levels where human relationships are most easily formed — at the level of physical attraction. Still others find their field of activity in the arts. Libra is ruled by the planet Venus and produces beautiful features and great charm. It is a symbol of culture and aesthetic refinement. It is seen at work wherever the factor of *form* operates as a means to bring scattered elements into cohesive patterns of order and beauty.

This factor of "form" is often little understood. Any kind of social organization, including industrial management, is based on the principle of form. Any relatively permanent relationship between two or more units means that a form or pattern has been constituted. The Night-force, in its operation throughout the Zodiac, depends upon form. There can be no "gathering together" without form. Every work of art is a formal gathering together

---

1 In Theosophy, the Brotherhood of the White Lodge is described as a hierarchy of adepts who have preserved the ancient truths and watch over and guide the evolution of humanity. "White" is associated not with race, but as an expression of "pure divinity." Annie Besant, "The White Lodge and it's Messengers," Theosophical Publishing House, Adyar, Madras. India May 1931.

and organization of separate units, whether these be pigments, lines, tones or physical materials; and so is a social group. Libra is the artist who dreams of ideal forms. Capricorn will make these ideal forms concrete and tangible among living men. The dream of the artist often inspires the politics of the statesman; witness Wagner's influence upon Hitler, who himself has a Libra Ascendant and is more an artist than a statesman — but has the power to inspire able statesmen.

Besides "form," another factor figures predominantly in the activities and reactions of the Libra type; and that is that of *evaluation*. This leads us to consider the symbol of the Scales associated with Libra. One should not take the symbol literally and conclude that Librans are "balanced" persons. They may be so occasionally; but just as often they will be found to be extremists in most important matters, even if ready seemingly to give in for the sake of social harmony.

The symbol of the Balance has actually a different meaning. Scales are used to weigh things. Weighing a thing is to compare its mass to that of a *socially accepted standard weight*. It is therefore to measure and to evaluate the fundamental character of a thing — its mass or weight — in terms of social value. Mass is fundamental, because it evaluates an object in terms of its relation to the planet as a whole, in terms of the factor of gravitation; and, moreover, because all values are estimated by reference to a certain wealth of gold. Scales, therefore, symbolize the evaluation of the most fundamental characteristics of any object. The point they emphasize is certainly not the factor of "balance" — a means to an end — but that of evaluation, measurement, and (on the basis thereof) of judgment.

The Libra type is essentially a person who evaluates things, people, events by referring them to fixed social standards, either traditional or ideal. He evaluates, and while he may not feel sure enough of his social standing to pass judgments "in the name of society" — as the Sagittarian will do remorselessly — nevertheless he will have weighed the evidence and fitted things very neatly where, in his view, they belong. To make his evaluations, Libra uses the main standards of social usefulness and the capacity to operate harmoniously in groups. They are social, and they are also aesthetic standards. And the Libran type often operates in the field of art, because it is *easier* to organize notes on a score, or lights and shades in a drawing, than to bring human personalities into stable patterns of organization.

Again, we must repeat that Libra is not yet a master of the social process. He has emerged out of the critical stage of self-examination and self-discipline stressed in Virgo. He has seen perhaps the Vision of the "ideal society," of the "New Jerusalem" — the perfect City or State. But it will take more stages of evolution before the power actually to build that State with men and women is developed. Thus, Libra dreams, evaluates, reaches toward and radiates the love which should eventually build the new group and the new society; but he does so as an artist rather than a politician — even though he may be a splendid manager. He is seer and harmonizer more than builder.

In another sense, Libra symbolizes the seed. It does so logically, because, in the seed, all the vital energies of the dying plant are gathered within a rigid form of organization. The seed is the symbol of the mystic brotherhood. It is also that of self-sacrifice. Thus, the first degree of Libra carries the symbol of the "butterfly impaled by a dart of wisdom." The chrysalis stage was that of Virgo. Virgo prepares in every way the ground for Libra. In Libra, the "new life" begins; life as a participant in the life of society, of any Greater Whole — be it Church or "White Lodge." Libra is the Initiate as he rises from the mystic sarcophagus in the King's chamber of the Pyramid. He has seen the Vision. He has recognized his place and function in his closest group as well as in the entire universe.

Now stretches before him the path of service to the group; but that service would be of little value indeed if the total reality of that greater whole was not experienced thoroughly by every part of himself. Thus, in Scorpio, that reality has to impregnate and revivify his feelings and emotions, the very substance of his personality; and in Sagittarius, it has to transfigure his mind. Libra's vision must be unsubstantiated in Scorpio; formulated mentally in Sagittarius. And as the winter solstice occurs, the Christ-child is born: God, or Humanity, become a man.

SCORPIO

The Scorpio phase of the yearly cycle of the life-force as it unfolds on earth and in human nature has been strangely misunderstood. Peculiarly negative attributes have been given to it as a result. They had to be negative because the interpreters failed to relate the Sign to the total cycle of the Day-force and the Night-force, stressing the ordinary individual's reaction to it at this stage of social evolution rather than the positive essence of the Sign itself; also because, with Scorpio, the coming of wintry days and long nights becomes evident, and primitive man resents this approach of physical darkness. He resents it, because he is rooted in the soil and a kin to vegetation and animal life. Scorpio brings tidings of hibernation; its frosts seal the doom of red and golden leaves. It has become, thus, the symbol of death. Only to a few could it mean "regeneration"; and even these few often did not realistically understand the meaning of such a regeneration.

While studying the symbolism of Libra, we stressed the fact that the three zodiacal Signs of the Fall period were steps in the growth of society and of the social consciousness in man. During this Fall period socializing forces are surging with ever increasing momentum following the increase in Power of the Night-force since the Fall equinox. The reality of human interchange, of living together within the organic, stable, permanent structure of a community is envisioned in Libra as a need and as an ideal of behavior. In Scorpio, this reality must be vitalized, made poignant and dramatic, inescapable. It must sink into the very flesh and glands of human beings; into their very depths and their very soul; into the substance of "personality." It must transform itself into a driving force. *That driving force is sex in its social aspects, sex as builder of civilization.*

The condemnation heaped upon Scorpio, "the accursed Sign," has paralleled the identification of sex and sin, which has conditioned so much of our Christian Western civilization. The subject, therefore, has become invaded by "complexes" and set attitudes, not easily transformed even by the most acute analysis. However, on the basis of a broad understanding of the complete zodiacal cycle of the Day-force and the Night-force much may be said which should bring light into many dark corners.

Sex has two basic aspects: procreative and non-procreative or social. The former corresponds to Taurus, the latter to Scorpio. That such a distinction has not been made by Western astrologers and philosophers is strange; for the correlation between Scorpio and the whole of sex-activity is very peculiar, considering that Scorpio is only a late Sign of the Zodiac and associated with autumn, the time when the life-force becomes somnolent in nature. Sex, as a strictly biological factor, is a primary function of all organisms and obviously should be associated with the animal mating season and the growth of flowers. It is symbolized by Taurus, the Bull — a hieroglyph of fertility and male strength.

Taurus is the sign of purely physiological and procreative mating. It is a phase of the process of personality-building. It represents late adolescence — its instinct toward unconscious procreation, its unsocial urge toward personal self-development through fecundating and being fecundated, thus, through sheer emotional experience. It witnesses the maximum emotional expression of the Day-force and of pure personality without any social context whatsoever. It is pure desire without mind or consciousness, without distortion or individual-social differentiation: a generic force which is universal and of itself has no "meaning." It just *is*; as life is.

The sign Scorpio is the polar opposite of Taurus. This means that, in the society building half-cycle of the Night-force's ascendancy, it occupies the same place occupied by Taurus in the personality-building half-cycle of the Day-force's ascendancy. To the Taurean mating urge corresponds, thus, another urge, which is Scorpio's essential characteristic. That urge is *the urge in the individual to merge in absolute union with other individuals in order to constitute together a greater organic whole.*

In Libra this urge is recognized as a motive for social conduct and group behavior; but in the very depth of the Libran's feelings there is still much individualism. The Day-force is too strong to allow the personality to let itself go completely into any union with others that would be irrevocable. Libra is a state of unstable equilibrium between a waning individualism and a waxing collectivism. But in Scorpio the desire to be a separate individual is being overwhelmed with *dramatic intensity* by the need to be more than oneself; by the urge to flow into others, as little streams merge into great rivers and rivers into the sea. That urge is the transcendent and social aspect of sex. It represents, not the procreative sex of late adolescence which warns to *build*, but the non-procreative, social and – yes — mystical sex of maturity which is a yearning for self-forgetfulness and union *through another* with a greater whole, and even with "God" — as the Orient and most "secret traditions" well understood.

Sex as a gate to "cosmic consciousness" has been known throughout the ages. Rituals have been devised to canalize this transcendental urge and lead it to its appointed goal. The Hindu Tantras and some forms of Yoga stress such rituals. All the temples of antiquity have witnessed them, and many Western societies have taught secretly practices which would lead to this merging of energies into a vaster reservoir of forces. Since the advent of Christianity, the subject has been shrouded in mystery and this is not the place to discuss this essence of all "practical occultism." But the reality of the zodiacal Sign Scorpio can never be understood until one realizes that the sex-force in Scorpio is not to be considered as a progeny-building force, but as a means to reach liberation from the narrow limits of self; to reach an ecstasy in which the individual becomes *more than himself*.

What does this "more" actually mean? The first concept such an ecstasy of union arouses in the consciousness is that of the "soul-mate": the One and the Other merged into a transcendent union "ordained by Life or God since Creation began." This is the Romantic ideal of union — an ideal which does not belong to the realm of Taurus and progeny-building mating, but which burns through Scorpio. It becomes entirely transcendent with the mystics who soar toward union with "the Beloved" — Life, God, the Master, or whatever name is given to that mystic "Other" with whom and in whom self loses its boundaries and cosmic consciousness is reached.

This, however, is only one aspect of that process of merging into a Greater Whole. The other is symbolized in Christianity by the union of the consecrated individual with the Church, the mystical Bride. Here we have the merging of the individual with the glorified community; a merging as poignantly intimate and emotionally fervent as the most perfect union of bodies and feelings. To know that the community exists, and to be eager to work for it, is Libra's realization. But in Scorpio there must be *identification*. Scorpio is the symbol of sex as psychic identification, with no thought of physical progeny — in fact, often in such a manner as to exclude the possibility of procreative results. In such psychic identification the Night-force triumphs — and the spiritual reality of civilization is born.

The home (Cancer) is built upon Taurus' procreative sex; but civilization (Capricorn) stems from Scorpio's social transformation of sex, *via* the mental generalizations and the social enthusiasms of Sagittarius. And here we touch upon the much discussed subject of culture *versus* civilization. Culture is rooted in the energies released in Taurus and in the Day-force; civilization, in the energies released in Scorpio and in the Night-force. Culture deals with particulars; civilization, with universals. Culture is based on traditions which are conditioned by climate, geography and inheritance of biological factors handed down from generation to generation. Civilization is the result of the work of creative geniuses and leaders who have fecundated the minds of countless human beings with their vision and their understanding. While civilization develops in the Sagittarius phase of the life-cycle, it has its roots in Scorpio. It has its roots in the urge, strong in all leaders of humankind, to pour of themselves unceasingly into the vast matrix of humanity.

That civilizing power is an aspect of the Scorpio type of sex, because it is born of the yearning to identify the self with the Greater Whole, humanity; to transcend oneself by fecundating society…and by being fecundated by divinity. That transcendent sexual activity bears a progeny; but it is a social progeny, a progeny of the spirit or the mind. And in that activity the Night-force operates, as, in Taurus, the Day-force sings through the fruitful mating of bodies.

There is nevertheless a negative side to this picture of release of power in Scorpio; a side provided by the waning Day-force which, then, has become more introverted and subjective, perhaps more subconsciously resentful in its action. It is the dark side of civilization: greed for social power and lust. That greed arises in the individual who, instead of merging himself into the greater whole, draws toward himself the energies produced by the living together, the human interchange of values and the commerce which are the foundations of society. Commerce, which is born — or at least permanently established — at the Libra level, generates abundant fruits in Scorpio. If these fruits are cornered by the greedy, then there is *social sin*. Every man who misuses the products of social interchange of values commits a sin against society. All big business trusts which are built on greed, all politicians who barter in public authority, all racketeers and gangsters, all leaders who play upon fear and mass-passions commit the sin of Scorpio. They lust for social power — instead of fecundating society as true civilizers, and of identifying their destinies with the destiny of their people.

The same is true of individuals who seek forever sexual pleasures and self-satisfaction. In these things, only the negative aspect of Scorpio is to be seen. The negative Day-force turns back to its own use the new energies produced by the molding power of the Night-force. It dreams, where it can no longer act. It creates pictures and temptations; it exacerbates desire. It produces sexual neuroses, where the yearning for merging into a greater stream of power through another human being — or through groups — is frustrated. Lust is born usually from a sense of defeat; just as criminals are often thwarted "men of action" who had it in themselves to fecundate society with their own genius.

Scorpio is no "accursed Sign," and sin or misery comes only where the great creative force is twisted and perverted by fears and complexes born of meaningless traditionalism disguised into virtue, or as a result of chaotic and vicious social conditions. It is where the free-play of energy in Taurus did not occur that the unfulfilled personality, when confronted with its new birth as participant in the life of society, recoils from the step represented by the positive Scorpio. Instead of that exalting union with others through which regeneration would come, a sense of frustration prevails which unfits the individual for that step. Resentment against society, or against the whole of life, prevails. And that resentment, that subconscious violence which would destroy the very means for liberation into the greater state, are to be symbolized by the stinging and poisonous Scorpio, in whose tail there is social and individual death.

It is not that the scorpion should be regenerated into the eagle, as symbolists are wont to say. The scorpion is a degeneration. It is not a natural product of healthy evolution. The eagle, or better still the phoenix, is a more adequate symbol of the reality of that phase of the natural cycle of yearly transformation which follows Libra. The phoenix symbolizes the birth of life at a new level through the burning of all limitations into the fire. This fire is the real symbol of the energy which burns in the man who has reached the eighth phase of his journey along the Zodiac. It is the fire which destroys lesser forms and summons greater ones to be developed during the Sagittarius period of the cycle. This fire is the transcendent and occult aspect of sex — which is very different from the instinctual procreative urge released in Taurus as a purely earthy and fruitful energy.

Much has been said about the thoroughness, ruthlessness, ambition, cruelty, jealousy and passion of persons in whose charts Scorpio is a dominant factor. But it is remarkable how many human beings, beside Scorpio types, display such characteristics and how often Scorpio natives fail to reveal them! Most of these negative traits in historical or living personalities are the direct results of *an archaic social state*. The Scorpio type constantly identifies himself with society, and society's passions are his passions. Society's ecstasy and glory would also be his ecstasy and his glory. He is a man in whom the energy of the social process flows with compelling intensity. If that energy is turned toward destruction, he becomes a superb destroyer; a ruthless chieftain or a criminal. When humanity will have learned to live as an organic whole, balanced, harmonious and healthy, then its Scorpio types will take on wings and commune with the Sun, as eagles indeed.

Scorpio is one of the four symbolic Gates through which *Avatars* are born; men who are the mouthpieces of the generic Father of the whole humanity, who is called "God." Scorpio symbolizes God's power as the supreme Civilizer of a united humankind; and it is significant that one whom millions have named "Avatar" and "Manifestation of God" was born in Scorpio: Baha'u'llah, the great Persian prophet who, less than a hundred years ago, proclaimed the Oneness of humanity through a new World-Order, and heralded the great age of organic humankind which will dawn.

SAGITTARIUS

With the Sign Sagittarius the Night-force, which increased in power since the summer solstice, is coming to its high-mark. The power that strove mightily through Libra and Scorpio to expand man's horizon and man's feelings is now operating almost unchallenged by the opposite trend of the Day-force, now at its lowest ebb. Collectivism overpowers individualism. Society dominates over personality; the far, over the near.

It is the age of great adventures into the vast unchartered realms of generalizations, of religion and philosophy, of abstraction and metaphysics. It is the time of Crusades and pilgrimages burning with the intensity of the quest for God, the quest for eternal values valid anywhere and at any time, the quest for absolutes. It is the age of social movements and of fanaticism, of martyrdom and intolerance; when men lose the sense of the earth, the narrow feelings of self-preservation and security, the will to personal happiness — and soar on the wings of self-denial toward distant social or mystical ideals, for which they are glad to die.

The logic of the process of development of social consciousness which asserted itself through Libra behavior and Scorpio emotions leads man, in Sagittarius, to new mental horizons. Whereas in the opposite zodiacal Sign, Gemini, man was trying eagerly to build a tight web of close connections — a nervous system, an intellectual system of logic, a technique of experiments to satisfy his curiosity about phenomena surrounding him — in Sagittarius the individual, completely absorbed by social or mystical factors, searches for *distant* connections. These connections will serve as the "nervous system" of the social organism, to the realization of which he is now dedicated. They will be, for instance, a network of telephonic and telegraphic lines; more abstractly still, a system of laws, ordinances, regulations which will enable the complex organism of society — the life of a city or nation — to operate satisfactorily.

Connections, close or distant, mean intelligence and mental activities. Thus, Gemini and Sagittarius are "mental" Signs. The former represents mind functioning within the lesser sphere of personality; the latter, mind operating within the greater sphere of society. In both cases the mental activities are direct and constructive. On the contrary, in Virgo (and we shall see later, in Pisces), the mind acts in a destructive, critical and, if all goes well, regenerative manner.

Mind, as the final stage of the rise of either the Day-force or the Night-force, is a builder. It synthesizes, extends and brings to their culmination and maximum radiance the energies of the Day and Night zodiacal tides. This is mind in the stages just before the solstices. But mind in the zodiacal Signs preceding the equinoxes is an entirely different kind of power. It is a power which clears up the stage for a new kind of activity, which denies and cleanses, which says constantly: "Not this! Not this!" It is mind telling you what should be forgotten, left behind, overcome and transcended. In Virgo, the personal emotionalism and the dramatic self-indulgence of Leo is to be curbed by self-discipline, hygiene, and self-immolation to a Teacher. In Pisces, it is the social excitement, the exaggerated idealism, the mystic fantasies and delusions of Aquarius which have to be analyzed away. The illusion of the "glory" of God must be transcended so that what the true mystics called the "poverty" of God, the silent and bare reality of the Presence of God, may be experienced in personality and in actuality.

In Sagittarius, man seeks to put *in working order* what he experienced with great depths of feelings in Scorpio. During the latter stage of his zodiacal journey the individual sought to merge with others in intimate and poignantly real union, that he might become more than himself and identify himself with the throbbing life of some greater organism. Greater organism may have meant at first the "Two-as-One" realization produced by the ecstasy of sex-fulfillment beyond any thought for progeny and self-reproduction. But the typical "greater organism" is the social group (or the occult Lodge), with the life of which the Scorpio type identifies himself in feelings, and of which he often becomes an unconscious mouthpiece — destructive or constructive according to the nature of the group's animating energies and purpose.

Scorpio is a Sign of power, and power seeks always a higher level from which it may be fed, in order that it may flow to a lower level at which it may operate as fecundator and ruler. In Sagittarius, power is already built in. Man *has* identified himself with the group — with society or any other kind of organic life vaster than his own. He has power to use. With that power he can build. By harnessing it he may travel far and wide.

In ancient symbolism we see Sagittarius represented by the Centaur, the mythical creature, half-horse and half-man, shooting his arrows heavenward. To say that the symbol describes a struggle between the human and animal natures is to say little — for the struggle between opposite energies goes on through the entire Zodiac. The real significance of the symbol is deeper and more precise. In every land, the horse represents virile power; but power of a special kind, power with which man can identify himself, which he can mount and with the help of which he can expand his range of activity. This he cannot do with the Bull's power, for the latter is unconscious, untamable, pure instinct — the power of cosmic Desire which man can kill by the sword (bull fights), but never consciously use for his own development. Taurus is therefore cosmic sex-power. Man is its tool, until he kills it by asceticism (the Buddha-symbol of energy overcoming).

Not so with the Sagittarius type of sex. That kind of power *can* be tamed and used. It becomes then symbolized by the *Horse*. Drinking the mare's milk gives great vitality — and is used for that purpose in Russia and Asia. Identifying oneself with the stallion's power is a worldwide symbol of becoming recharged with power for use — whether it be destructive use (Genghis Khan's "Golden Hordes" riding on their fierce Mogul horses) or constructive use. The Sagittarius type therefore *has* become identified with power — power that burns in the "groins" and is centered, *in Yoga*, in the region of the solar plexus; a fact which the psychoanalyst also recognizes as he interprets dreams of horses of various colors. Half of Sagittarius is "power"; the other half is "he who uses power" — that is, the conscious mind of man. A third attribute (bow and arrows) refers to direction and purpose. The Centaur shoots *upward* at a 45° angle, symbol of the maximum mobilization of energies.

The centaurs were sons of Gaia, the Earth. In other words, they were the products of an identification with the energies of that greater organism, the planet. In Sagittarius, man, having identified himself with the power generated by society and by the complex interchange between human beings (sex, business, commerce, art, propaganda, etc.), has become "power-full." *His problem is how to direct it in the proper channels.* The Sagittarian's problem does not refer essentially to a struggle between two *natures*; it deals with a choice of *directions* for the power which has been built in within his "groins." And the Centaur symbolism indicates what the correct direction is, by the angle at which the Centaur shoots his arrows.

The Sagittarius type is occupied mainly with "working efficiency" and direction. He is the typical manager of power; the "man-agent" of power. For the manager is the person who directs and organizes the release of power for maximum efficiency and minimum waste; also, for greatest speed and greatest reach. On the other hand, the typical "executive" is developed essentially in Capricorn, because the executive is the symbol of the working organization as a whole, in its relation to society as a whole. He is the center and symbol of the State. Sagittarius is the Prime Minister; Capricorn, the King or Emperor — and Aquarius, the Reformer.

The Sagittarian mentality is a very coherent and cohesive kind of mentality — thus its stubborn and unyielding quality. It sees everything in terms of "schedule of operation" or law. It is also, at another level, completely obsessed by ethics; but ethics as a working system of human relationship and not as an idealist's dream. The Sagittarian is not primarily an idealist. He wants to extend that which is; to organize it and make it work by finding all possible connections between every part of the whole and by seeing them operate properly. He is interpreter, rather than inventor of new goals. He codifies. He finds new meanings, new dimensions of thinking. He clears up obscure points. He pierces through veil after veil. But he does not lose himself, like the Scorpio and even more the Aquarius type, into wild identifications with boundless energies or mystical realizations. He never surrenders the sense of boundaries, of form, of a definite rhythm of operation. He is not Eagle, but Horse. His power stems from the reality of the known and the experienced. He may shoot arrows at the stars, but his feet remain on the earth, which he loves because it is the source of his power.

It is the source of his power; but he is not bound to it. *He uses it.* He manages its power. He treats it well, just as a Mogul warrior or a nomad treats well his horses; merely because he knows he is dependent upon it for maximum efficiency, in fact for his very life. Therefore, the Sagittarian is keen on exercising his body and muscles, on feeling the soil under his feet; keen also on working with people, in getting the feel of society; despondent and fretful if alone, or (in the less mental type) if confined in a narrow environment. He needs open space, large rooms. He loves to organize other people's lives — with often unpleasant results! He loves to handle power and to speed.

In modern life the automobile and the tank are taking the place of the horse. What is the source of their power? Oil deep in the "bowels of the earth." And so, leaders like Churchill and General de Gaulle who were the first to recognize the value of the tank in modern warfare are Sagittarians; and so, the birth-chart of the United States, the land of the automobiles, outdoors and sports, has most likely Sagittarius rising.

At a higher level, we find Sagittarius associated with religion; but only with *organized* religion and rituals. Religion, as an organized social force, is born of the individual's yearning for psychic identification with the wholeness of the community's life. It is a communal enterprise, powered by men's yearning to feel collectively united. Priests and theocratic rulers are the managers of that communal energy. The Prophet gives form to it. He creates "images of salvation," symbols of unification. He projects himself as such a symbol. He becomes a mythical Personage, a Solar Hero. He is the soul of the community. He is humanity condensed into One Perfect Man; the projection of the very Fatherhood of God.

As to the philosopher and metaphysician — also a product of Sagittarian activity — such a one is he who establishes workable order in the midst of the bewildering complexity of social and natural phenomena. He does this by recognizing all sorts of hidden connections and correlations between events; by interpreting and formulating generalizations in terms of laws. He travels in the "realm of Ideas." But he travels with the use of the power he released by identifying himself *with the need of his group*. Nothing has more significance to the higher type of Sagittarian than the "need of the times," the need of the community to which he belongs. To realize that need and to become identified with it are the very sources of his power as a thinker, seer and formulator. He is that need having taken form and name. He is interpreter, reader of omens and "signs of the times," planner, prophet and seer. But what he "sees" is what there is a *social need* for him to see. He is the servant of the community.

On the negative side of the picture, we find the Sagittarian as a fanatic and as a Puritan (and the Puritan background of the American tradition again stresses a Sagittarian Ascendant for the United States). Just because the personalizing energy of the Day-force is at its lowest ebb in Sagittarius, the native of that sign has very little regard for individuals. He willingly sacrifices anything personal and individualistic to the altar of the "good of the community." The Spanish Inquisition is a typical Sagittarian product (Spain is ruled by Sagittarius), for it tortured the individual personality to save the soul. It sacrificed the near to the far. Scorpio's frustrations may also lead to Sagittarian fanaticism, which then becomes more violent and cruel through sadistic features. The community accordingly has not only the right to save itself at the cost of its individuals' sufferings and deaths; the man who claims the right to manage that religious-social power finds a perverse exaltation in the torture. Thus, personal asceticism (deliberate or enforced) leads to cruelty.

The Sagittarian has so vague an objective and positive sense of individualism and, on the other hand, such an overwhelming social sense, that he has, at times, to resort to subconscious subterfuges and to the thrill of violence in order to get back a feeling of his own personality. In fact, he does this rather often as a rule, especially as the chaos of medieval and modern society fills him with destructive energies. Thus, the Sagittarian may seem on the surface to be a boisterous individual and an arrogant personality. This, again, is due to his very surrender to non-individualistic forces. The Day-force at its lowest point of power has to strain itself in order to give to itself the illusion of strength. It needs "strong meat" to be aroused, and when aroused it acts at times in archaic and compulsive ways which are just as unpleasant as the negative Scorpio traits, and perhaps more dangerous because more sharpened by intellectual mechanisms. Then Jupiterian compassion becomes more or less unconscious sadism.

Sagittarius is the prelude to Christmas. As the snow, it absorbs all littleness into the vast womb of silence from which the new birth of the Day-force will emerge. The mind that binds all life into patterns of cosmic relationships has become a "mother of the Living God." The Sagittarian has all the heroisms, the self-abnegation and the loving tyranny of mothers. He closes an era and opens another. He is pregnant with divinity.

CAPRICORN

The time of the winter solstice has now come, opening the Gates of Capricorn. The days have decreased in length as much as they ever will. Long wintry nights absorb nature in their repose, as snow covers the ultimate disintegration of living things with its vast expanse of peace and quietude. Death seems to rule supreme over the visible universe. And yet, somewhere and forever, a new Christ is born. Life surges once more with the Sun from its southern decline. The Sun moves northward, its daily arc of light becomes slowly tauter and more radiant. The promise of spring spreads like a mystic fire over the earth to tell "men of good will" that the New Life has begun to win over arrested death.

What is this new life which men have symbolized in the beautiful Christ-story, whose roots go deeply into the soil of older mythologies? Who is the eternal *Christos*, whose significance remains everlastingly true and vital, whether or not men believe in the historical or religious Christ? It is the "Day-force"; that aspect of the bi-polar life-force which, as a *personalizing* energy, tends to transform the scattered and disintegrated remains of a previous cycle into a new organic whole, integral because defined by limitations, creative because conscious. That new organic whole in the realm of humankind is what will grow in time into the fulfilled personality: that is, the human individual, conscious of his relative uniqueness, centered in the sense of his "I-am-ness," in an ego. The Christos is that power in the universe which leads men to "individuation." It is the foundation upon which all concepts of equality and democracy, of the abstract value of the individual, of the dignity and intangibility of the human personality, are based. It is the foundation of the "self-evident truths" of the Declaration of Independence, the center of the "Rights of Man."

The Christos is the universal energy of the Day-force during its period of ascendancy through winter and spring. It is "born" at the winter solstice, because, from that day onward, it increases at the expense of its polar opposite, the Night-force, which thenceforth begins to decline. The Night-force is an in-gathering, *collectivizing* energy. It expands personality into society through the magic of human relationships. It begins with the building of the family, at the symbolical summer solstice, in Cancer, the sign of the home. It extends progressively the sphere of this family through the zodiacal phases of Virgo and Libra. It glorifies man's responsibility to his progeny and man's participation in all social groups. It impels the individual to seek an ever deeper identification with ever larger collectivities. It brings to man the generalizations and the discoveries of civilization, whose development binds together generation to generation, racial group to racial group, individual achievement to individual achievement — until personalities discover themselves to be but relatively insignificant cells in the vast organism of human society. Tribal groups and small nations ultimately disappear. The days of the empire have come. The State rules supreme; and its symbol of power, Caesar, multiplies itself in effigy through the ubiquitous and all-corrupting power of money.

Caesar and the Christos: both of them operate through the zodiacal field of Capricorn. Caesar is at the apex of his power; Christ is only a hunted baby. Yet Caesar's empire will soon collapse, and the power of the Christos will wax ever stronger through Aquarius and Pisces, until it arises as an irresistible challenge of life and personality with the coming of spring and the ascendancy of the Day-force in Aries.

In Capricorn, the individual power of the human personality is seeking its way out, struggling from under the great weight of the State. The Night-force triumphs. Society is seen as an ultimate in that vast collective organism, the State, which dominates even its leaders. The great flights of civilization soaring through Sagittarius on the wings of the philosophical, scientific and social mind have now reached a point of crystallization. Perceivers of the beyond are superseded by organizers of empire. Ever shifting and remote boundaries must be watched and fortified by armies and administrators. The central authority must establish rigid patterns of government so as to hold under its impersonal rule many and diverse races, many trends of thought, many traditions.

The imperial Rome of the Caesars is no longer the original citadel of Roman citizens, the sturdy and vigorous Rome of earlier days. It is a sprawling metropolis, a universal city. Likewise, when a man has passed successfully through the evolutionary periods represented by Scorpio and Sagittarius, he is no longer the direct and aggressive ego hiding his social uncertainties under big dramatic gestures. The ego has expanded by becoming established in social groups, through partnerships of all kinds, through identification with the strange and wondrous powers which rise from all collectivities, from their ancient past, from that reservoir of unfathomable energy which has been called the Collective Unconscious.

This Collective Unconscious, time after time, has flooded the merely personal ego with intoxicating powers released by non-procreative sex and by civilization. Either the human person has become the tool of such powers, passively submitting to lust and the hectic rhythm of city-life; or else he has mastered these powers. He has become adept in Scorpio and philosopher in Sagittarius. His ego, then, instead of expanding into a power-greedy monstrosity ceaselessly avid for more lust, or more knowledge, or more money, has undergone a basic metamorphosis. It has surrendered its energy to a greater center of organization and of consciousness, which is the Self — the center of both the conscious sphere and the vast Unconscious around it.

Centered in his ego, a human person is but a limited and narrow organism of life and consciousness. He is, symbolically, a small tribe, a small State. He is separate from all other personalities. His Leo pride is a perpetual bondage. His creative gestures are rooted but in the small realm of his personal experience and his own geographical surroundings. But when man ceases to refer every feeling, every valuation, every thought to the center of his own narrow being; when man, through social interchanges and through love, through education and world-understanding, through commerce, travel and planet-wide contacts, succeeds in *assimilating* the vast contents of the civilized world of his time — then he must discover another center of reference; he must accept another framework of consciousness to hold all he has obtained. The "fortified castle" of his ego is left behind and he moves his residence to the "metropolis" of his greater Self. However, it also may be that by making such a move away from his small center of power, he becomes a mere attendant at the court of some powerful Emperor, a passive participant in the greatness and the glory of the empire.

The growth of a small tribe into a vast empire, like the Roman Empire, parallels most accurately the unfoldment of a personality from his narrower sense of ego and his individual pride to the condition where either the man becomes a master of greater life, or a passive participant in some vast power-group from which he absorbs knowledge, sustenance and power in reflected glory.

Capricorn symbolizes thus any typical State-organization encompassing large territories and various racial groups, and all that goes with such an organization, especially politics and the play of power. It symbolizes also in the individual human being that mysterious stage of being and consciousness, of which the perfected Hindu *Yogi* is the most characteristic representative: viz. the man who, though he lives alone, has made of his personality a vast cosmos over which he exercises a special kind of control, and, though he be a mendicant, is rich with the wealth of all society and a participant in the power and glory of transcendent Hosts. Nevertheless, Capricorn represents also the courtier who worships at the shrine of some potentate and receives crumbs of power, and the modern politician (or bureaucrat) who is a little wheel in a big machine draining vitality from the State which it is meant to serve.

In Cancer, the personality finds the consummation of its selfhood in becoming completed by a permanent partner and definitely established in a home; yet this consummation contains also the seed of that which will ultimately overcome the individual ego. The triumph of society over personality lurks in the conjugal embrace which, at the time, seems to the man but an exaltation of self and of the powers of self.

Likewise in Capricorn, society and all the collectivizing forces of life seem to triumph in the establishment of the powerful State. There also the individual man, having assumed a profession and a particular social function, seems to have consolidated himself forever in this function. But such Capricornian achievements have in themselves the germ of their destruction. Behind any perfected State stands the impending and unavoidable Revolution. No professional achievement is stable because society is not a static entity, and, out of the constantly moving flux of social relationships and social opportunities, challenges to any established order must arise from new generations, from new inventions, from new materials conquered but not assimilated.

The Capricornian State cannot be set; because it is, by definition, built on far and forever expanding factors, on credit and commerce, on metaphysical speculations which are not susceptible of concrete proofs, and on religious organizations which must be destroyed by the very men who take their beliefs most to heart and incorporate them in their lives: mystics and saints. A small tribal organism can persist for millennia because it is so concrete; because the value of its regulations is evident, and its blood-unity is incontrovertible. But an empire *must* keep shifting its boundaries; politicians *must* make compromises and bargains with those who, aroused to a taste of power, will want constantly more and will destroy their leaders. The wealthy, in order to increase their wealth, *must* educate the masses into becoming both technicians to handle machines and consumers to absorb the machines' products. And the masses, thus educated, will rise. Civilization — the Capricornian god — must forever destroy itself while increasing its scope and its powers. Its noblest children are the very ones who will be the leaders in this destruction: the reformers and dreamers, these minds whom no achievement can ever satisfy. They will carry in their souls the signature of Aquarius.

Why, however, must these Aquarian reformers feel so deeply dissatisfied with the *status quo*, so eager for transformation and revolution? Because within their depths of as yet unconscious being the newly awakened Day-force stirs. And the destruction of the old, which they may engineer, is but the operation of that "sword" which the Christ told us he came to bring: "not peace, but a sword." The Aquarian reformer follows the lead of the Capricornian seer. What he voices is indeed the power of a new human type born within the unconscious depths of the Empire, the power of submerged classes which, having been stirred by their masters into consciousness or into greed, are fated to rise.

This new human type is the Christos, born at the winter solstice in the "manger" — in the cradling depths of unconscious humankind, hardly aware beyond animality. It is a new type of personality, a new type of home. Both will be completed only during the coming Cancer period, but they begin to take form within the motherly peace of the snow that covers the vast seed-potential of the earth. Just as society becomes eventually, in its imperial State, what was formed in seed in the conjugal embrace, likewise the individual personality in its glory can be traced to that seed which was sown at the apex of the once great Empire "among the sheep and the goats": the Christos-seed. That seed is the source of the Day-force. It is the well-spring of "living waters" — of those "living waters" which will be poured abundantly from the urn of Aquarius, the Water-bearer.

In Capricorn, the Christos-seed is almost entirely unnoticeable, so completely overwhelmed is the renascent Day-force by the vast structure built by the Night-force. It is to be seen only in the heart of the Capricornian *Yogi* or Seer; the recluse Hermit; the lonely Wanderer on the heights of snow-covered peaks; the solitary Individual, who, after having assimilated within the strong structure of his selfhood the total contents of the Collective Unconscious, has become a "womb of human totality." In that "womb" which represents the fulfillment of an entire cycle of human expansion, he who has become a *seed-man* receives in utter consecration the New Life that comes from on high. Nine months have elapsed since prolific nature became impregnated by the Sun in Taurus. Nature is thus ready for the birthing of the New Type.

This is the mystery that dwells within the unconscious depths of the noblest among natives of Capricorn. They bear within themselves a living seed; yet know not yet the meaning of that seed. And in despair of loneliness and frustration they seek forgetfulness in social activities, social sins and intoxicants. They crave power, yet power fails to satisfy — and they know it. So, they seek lust and eccentricities to soothe their emptiness. They are called "selfish," because they wear a mask. And they dare not let go of the mask, for fear they would have to see their social stature and their ambitions crumble while worshipping the new babe within their souls.

A typical Capricornian was Woodrow Wilson — whom intuitives have identified with the ancient Pharaoh Akh-na-ton, who was the first to promulgate in the Western world a transcendent monotheism, a new religion of the One God which he forced upon his unwilling people, and which was destroyed after his death. Likewise, Wilson attempted to force upon his people his lofty international idealism, his vision of united humankind. In the Egypt of the XIVth century B.C. religious monotheism represented the New Type of human consciousness. Today, the Federation of Humanity is the promise of, and foundation for the new Man. And a noble Capricornian, with all the faults and the loneliness of a Capricornian, attempted to bring to men the realization of that new birthing of Reality — and failed because his people could not see above their inertia and their politicians. Now an Aquarian is taking up the burden of the New Life.

In due time the New Life always wins. The new type of human being pierces through the crust of the decaying matter of what was once the powerful State erected by Caesar, as spring impels seeds to germinate after the Piscean deluge of equinoctial storms. The Christos always wins against Caesar. The Federation of Man must win over the imperial machines erected by power-groups using Sagittarius energies — machines and propaganda, tanks and fanaticism — to crystallize their ambition. The cycle of life does not allow static fulfillment. Everything turns into its opposite. The wheel moves on everlastingly and the Day-force interplays with the Night-force in an ever-renewed drama which is life itself.

AQUARIUS

With Aquarius, we reach the last of the "fixed Signs"; the Signs through which *power is released*. Power is energy ready for purposeful use through instrumentalities prepared for it. The nature of the power depends upon the character of the energy to be used; thus "fixed" zodiacal Signs follow "cardinal" Signs, and as there are two basic types of cardinal Signs — those which start with the equinoxes (Aries and Libra) and those which start with the solstices (Cancer and Capricorn) — likewise there are two basic types of succeeding fixed Signs.

We can thus speak of equinoctial power (Taurus and Scorpio) and of solstitial power (Leo and Aquarius). Equinoctial power is conditioned by the intense dynamism of the equinoctial Signs, Aries and Libra — Signs of maximum speed of the Sun's motion in declination; Signs in which the Day-force and the Night-force are most evenly balanced. Solstitial power is the outcome of a strong, concrete type of activity during the solstitial periods (Cancer and Capricorn) which begin with the Sun's motion in declination reduced to a minimum speed and which see the triumph respectively of the Day-force and the Night-force.

Where the cardinal Sign displays intense dynamism and instability, the succeeding fixed Sign must, as it were, arrest this dynamic activity and limit it. Thus, Taurus puts to organic use, and forces into concrete purposes, the impetuous and universalistic energy of Aries; and Scorpio brings the often diffused social eagerness of Libra to a state of stubborn identification with a particular purpose or a particular person (whence jealousy, cruelty and the like). On the other hand, when the cardinal Sign shows focalization upon either personality (Cancer) or a particular form of society (Capricorn), the power demonstrated by the fixed Sign which follows manifests as a release or as an outburst of energy.

This release either expands and glorifies what has been built and focalized in the cardinal Sign, or else tends to destroy and transcend it. Thus, a release of power in Leo may mean the disruption of the home and of personal integrity through love affairs, gambling and intemperate gestures, as well as the building of a progeny which consolidates the home. Likewise, Aquarius may see the constructive development of State and civilization through inventions, social improvements and the glorification of special social virtues. It may also mean revolution and a complete upheaval of State and civilization by the power of a new type of human being and of new ideals which the existing State blindly refuses to tolerate, or against which it must fight because it cannot possibly assimilate it.

This distinction between equinoctial and solstitial characteristics is of the greatest importance, if the more vital meaning of the Zodiac is to be understood. It finds also its expression in the traditional zodiacal terminology which states that the equinoctial cardinal Signs (Aries and Libra) are "masculine," and the succeeding fixed Signs (Taurus and Scorpio) "feminine"; while the solstitial cardinal Signs (Cancer and Capricorn) are "feminine" and the succeeding fixed Signs (Leo and Aquarius) "masculine." Feminine fixed power-Signs concentrate and focalize masculine cardinal activity-Signs; thus, Taurus is solar power impregnating the earth, and Scorpio is the power of human relationship and of social partnership fixed respectively in sexual identification and in business or in trusts. On the other hand, masculine power-Signs release what has been made concrete, or what has become crystallized, in feminine activity-Signs; thus, Leo symbolizes creative and procreative power released from the formed personality and the established home, and Aquarius represents civilization expanding or reforming itself through its inventors, seers and revolutionists.

In Capricorn, the individual man is a politician, a social automaton, or a hermit in travail of a new vision. In Aquarius, the individual may be a rebel or a true reformer, a crank stubbornly trying to peddle his personal scheme of social improvement, or the devotee of a new religion which may renew vast groups of men. He may go to social martyrdom with the same passionate obstinacy with which a Leo person takes violent pride in his own creations or clings to his theatrical emotions. He is the social man trying passionately to cease being a mere creature of the State and to pour his ineradicable sense of bondage to tradition into a specialized social group consecrated to reform — any reform. He is the Party-man who is never more faithful to his Party than when the latter is attacked by conservatives or persecuted by the State as a whole. He is the fanatic who has no individualistic steering wheel to help him direct rationally his fanaticism. But he is also the Edison who fulfills a social order through his inventive genius, and the Liberator who saves a people from bondage and renews civilization without destroying its basic structure. He may pour new wine in old bottles, or break the old bottles and spill the wine for lack of adequate containers.

It is fashionable these days to sing the praise of the noble Aquarian. This is understandable because humankind is passing through a period of swift transition and social repolarization. The feudal and bourgeois structures of European civilization are being shattered by the attacks of aroused destroyers. People feel the need of the change, even if their conscious minds resist it desperately. That Capricornian conservatism is doomed, everyone in his senses knows; but the privileged class and the guardians of religious traditions cannot let go of the keys to an order, the destruction of which obviously must mean their destruction and temporary chaos. In Europe, war is achieving what revolution began; but in America the issue between reform or revolution seems still to be open. Reform in the hands of the finest Aquarians would mean a return to the breadth of vision of Sagittarian America, to her moral sense and her healthful eagerness for big adventures and religious dreams. Revolution would mean that Sagittarian values in America have become so crystallized in the hands of negative Capricornians, that nothing but the destruction of these shells can enable us to discover the "still, small voice" of the Christos, of the New Life.

Why "Sagittarian" values? Because it is in Sagittarius that universal Principles and social, religious Ideals are envisioned by the mind that soars beyond personal racial and geographical realms and into the sphere of the most distant connections and generalizations. And what is Democracy and the principle of a universal Brotherhood of Man if not the most extreme generalization which man can make about human relationship? Tribal Law — even in its expanded Nazi meaning — is based on proximate connections, on personal and emotional experience. But the Democratic Law does violence to our archaic instincts, rooted as they are in blood exclusivism and cultural pride.

No wonder then, that, as the modern Sagittarian ideal of Democracy crystallizes into Capricornian politics, most of the old ancestral hatred and class-prejudices tend to regain the ground they have occupied for ages. With Democracy (and all it implies fundamentally in terms of human relationship, rather than superficially in terms of the parliamentary system) the Sagittarian mind reaches beyond the previous highest level of generalization represented by the universal Catholic Order. Catholicism means etymologically, universalism. Christianity was based on the supreme human generalization that every human being was potentially a "Son of God." That generalization, however, became restricted and crystallized into a Church which set boundaries to spiritual salvation and provided hell-fires for all unbelievers. These Capricornian boundaries became symbolized by the Papacy and the medieval Roman Church — and they eventually called for reformers and rebels to break them down.

Democracy, in the broadest and deepest sense of the term, is a still vaster generalization because it is not limited to the religious and ethical sphere, but takes hold of every value of human behavior and repolarizes them until all blood distinctions, all emotionalism in human relationship, all sense of possessiveness based on ancestral connotations, are uprooted. Democracy, being an ideal, has to become concrete as an applied system of social-political organization. As this happens, Sagittarian values are superseded or dominated by Capricornian technique. Ideal Democracy becomes applied Federalism. What the United States has demonstrated during its 170 years of existence is a hesitant and unreliable sense of Democracy and a stubborn dependence upon the often twisted and perverted mechanisms of Federalism. We have taken for granted that parliamentarism means Democracy, that the respect for majority decisions in any elected group of representatives proves that Democracy operates. This is obviously naïve, as all depends upon *how* elections are conducted and whether financial, social and psychological pressure is, or is not, applied to force a decision of the electorate.

With Capricorn, we see therefore the triumph of political machines, of personal dictatorship on the basis of special techniques of control of public opinion. We see the human personality, developed through the cycle of the ascendancy of the Day-force, now becoming the "forgotten individual": the man with a vote that can be bought or directed by emotional mass-appeals. And in Aquarius we see, on one hand, the constructive and destructive release of all the powers which modern city life can produce in the way of material comfort and technology, or in the way of mental confusion, moral pollution and physiological disintegration — and on the other hand, the many attempts of the "citified" man to reestablish his individual sense of values and his personal integrity by small or big rebellions, by eccentricities, by one-sided emotional fanaticisms, by allegiance to cults and specialized groups. In the name of "going back" to the "law of Nature" (vegetarianism, raw-foodism, nudism, etc.) or to the "law of individualistic Democracy" (anarchistic ideologies of one type or another), or to the "law of Universal Brotherhood" (spiritual, esoteric groups) the "citified" man seeks to revivify the Sagittarian vision which Capricornian metropoles and Capricornian power-groups have betrayed. Thus, the Aquarian's yearning for the unfamiliar and the foreign, for the newest fads or for the movements which are supposed to revive and restore the "true" foundation of Democracy and human freedom.

In all such attempts toward liberation from the social machine and the domination of money and power-groups, the Aquarian displays most often a peculiar reliance upon the very social forces he would condemn. This must be so, because all he really knows is social action and social organization. His sense of personality is still very vague or most negative. In Aquarius, the "personalizing" energy of the Day-force is as yet very weak and barely able to operate. It operates at best fitfully and often through mere reaction against other personalities who are parts of a social situation.

Just as the Leo person makes *big social gestures* in order to hide his deeply hidden sense of social insecurity or his "inferiority complex," likewise the Aquarian makes *big personal gestures* in order to hide his usually unacknowledged sense of personal insecurity and his fear of any strong personality. Fear of course can, under favorable circumstances, turn into devotion; but not a little resentment may lurk in the shadow of this devotion, not a little hope of somehow proving himself superior to the object of the devotion.

The Aquarian feels in his innermost depth the presence of a New Life; but he is often frightened by the implications of such a presence. It might force him to give up his reliance upon social background. It might compel him to be truly an individual and to prove it to himself by a completely unemotional peace rooted in nothing but that "still, small voice" which is, as yet, barely anything but a presentment and a disturbing promise. And, indeed, the Aquarian does not want to give up his reliance upon his social and ancestral background — except for theatrical exhibitions of "modernism" which merely add to his prestige with friends. Moreover, the plunge into the depths of his personality is a fearsome venture, because individual selfhood means very little to him in the way of security. To be an individual secure in one's selfhood — that ideal evokes only as a rule an intellectual assent. Fundamentally, the Aquarian is just as afraid of being himself, independently of all social and cultural props, as the Leo leader is afraid of being merely a "social being" without the privileged personal position of leading whomsoever he is being "social" with.

Lincoln defined the true democrat as one who "refuses to be a master of slaves." But the Leo type wants to be the leader of his social group because he fears to function socially in any other capacity; and, most of all, as an equal among equals. The typical Aquarian can operate as an equal among equals, for he is at ease in society; he can also use freely whatever social power is his by ancestral tradition and social consent. But he really depends upon a social status and a legal (or fictitiously legal) status to give himself the sense that *society needs him*. He has to feel that he is a "man of destiny" for those he will lead; whereas the Leo ruler glories merely in being a ruler, because he wants to rule and in ruling he feels he has made his adjustment to society. An Aquarian may sincerely renounce power and, if need be, abdicate; the Leo type will do so only if he thinks that by such a noble gesture he will gain more social prestige than by holding on to a throne which seems insecure.

Where the Capricorn-organized collectivity comes close to being an ideal society, the Aquarian may emerge from it as the representative of its perfect organic wholeness. In this case he becomes the plenipotentiary of the group, or the seed which, leaving the fulfilled parent organism, is the embodiment of all its vital power. In Aquarius the power of the Christ-seed is released into the new virgin soil; this seed will germinate in due time and become lost as a seed so that the new plant may be.

In that sense, the great men who, having assimilated in their personality all the most progressive trends of European culture, came to the "New World" and identified themselves with its civilization, presenting to America the gifts of their European wisdom and personality, acted as *seed-men* and symbolically speaking, as true "Aquarians." The ideal Capricorn is the "Divine City" or "White Lodge," whose "birthday" is celebrated early in January, at the opposite pole of the year from the date of the Declaration of Independence; a significant symbol indeed.[2] And the "Aquarians" of the Spirit are those mysterious Personages who cyclically go forth from that "Divine City" — the Pleroma of God — to release therefrom the "Living Waters" of the New Life.

Thus, the Aquarian symbolism of the Water-Bearer, who carries on his shoulder an "urn" whence flows down

---

[2] See earlier note under Libra section about theosophy's "White Lodge" concept. "White City" has been changed to "Divine City" here for better readability. The "White City" refers to another concept from theosophy that Rudhyar was familiar with. As reported by The San Diego history center, "In 1897, Katherine Tingley established the Universal Brotherhood and Theosophical Society on the Point Loma peninsula in San Diego, California. Under her leadership, this dusty seaside plot of land—popularly known as Lomaland—was transformed into a lush, vibrant "White City" that became a center of learning and culture."

to the earth a stream of water. This urn is a symbol of the mystic seed-bag, releasing the substance of a new humanity. It is also a symbol of the storm-cloud, laden with bountiful rain which will water the expectant crop, and releasing the lightning — which the old Aryans deified as *Rudra*. The lightning is not only a destructive force. It is the means for the precipitation out of the air of precious nitrogen necessary to living processes.

Power flows always from a higher to a lower potential, from the fulfilled to the yet incomplete or the expectant. Power in Aquarius can be, perhaps more truly than in any other fixed Sign of the Zodiac, the Power of God. Thus, the Divine Manifestation for the "Aquarian Age" is expected by some to be the most powerful outpouring of creative Spirit. Perhaps that outpouring is even now flooding the human realms. Perhaps the Archetypal Man has already taken flesh and blood, and men's minds are soon to behold the fullness and the glory of the Revelation that shall be made concrete by many who will come from the celestial "Divine City," as seed for the new humanity.

This is the promise of Aquarius, whose "living waters" flow from celestial heights to impregnate the human kingdom as a totality for a new birth of Personality — for the birthing of the "Man of Plenitude" in our children and our children's children.

PISCES

The last stage of the Sun's zodiacal journey is reached in Pisces as the Day-force, steadily waxing stronger, prepares to balance and overcome the waning Night-force. The Christ-seed, which was activated at the winter solstice in the hidden depths of a world utterly dominated by social behavior and by the concept of the State, has now unfolded to the point where it has to be recognized by a society breaking down under the weight of its crystallizations. The once-powerful Empire is attacked from all sides by waves of destructive energy, by the rip-tide of Barbarian invasions. New blood is flowing into the old ruling classes, utterly transforming them. The proud "isolationists" are swept away when they refuse to link themselves up to the rising crest of the spring-to-be — as wintry icebergs are sent to liquid deaths by the equinoctial storms which rage through the Piscean period.

Pisces is an era of storms and of wholesale disintegration. But Piscean winds of destiny may impel men of vision and courage to discover many a "new world," as much as they do destroy or suffocate the many who stubbornly resist change. Pisces is an era of often sharp and violent repolarization. It is an era of purgation and cleansing. Tradition has made of the month preceding the vernal equinox a period of fasting and repentance. Beginning with Ash Wednesday, the devotee of the New Life must learn to identify himself willingly with the death of all established structures. He must be willing to face the chrysalis state for the sake of the butterfly-to-be. Pisces is the mythical Deluge and the age of universal dissolution. Man must accept structural dissolution under the insidious power of Neptune, ruler of Pisces. He must cling to no stability or no past greatness. "No-security" is for him the only possible security. He must learn to operate in terms of the waxing Day-force and to stand unmoved while the structures built by the Night-force are shattered all around him.

In the opposite Sign, Virgo, the individual, having proudly released in Leo the energies of his personality, is confronted by the results of such releases. His progeny must be cared for. His creative works may show failings and inadequacies. His health may have been impaired by passional excesses; his patrimony may have been squandered through useless speculation. In Virgo, the individual faces this need of repolarizing his emotional attitude as well as of improving his technique of behavior. Self-criticism, study, hygiene and discipleship to a "master of technique" are therefore his needs. By satisfying them he begins to get a new perspective upon human relationships. He learns to serve, to have patience, to listen, to meditate and to criticize the most basic impulses of his personality. If he does not learn willingly, he may be compelled by illness or servitude to open himself to the true life of human relationship and to become in Libra — a "social" being.

With Pisces we find the winds of destiny turned to the opposite point of the compass. Here it is the "social" man who must learn to give up his comfortable, or even his tragic, reliance upon the structure of society. He must learn to stand alone and to rely only upon his own inner Voice. He must be willing to "close accounts" and face the unknown with simple faith; to re-enter the womb of nature, leaving behind the beautiful mirages of the Aquarian civilized life and bracing himself for life in the wilderness of some greater realm, for long voyages to a new world. He must learn to un-learn and to give up even his set ideals and his possessions. He must learn even, as mystics do, to pierce through the wondrous sphere of the "glory of God" and to search, undaunted, through the darkness of human consciousness for the "poverty of God," that hidden state where there is silence and nothing, yet whence all things that have form and name emanate in the stillness of the supreme Mystery.

In Virgo, the proud personality must learn to be an apprentice and to serve a master. But, in Pisces, the social man who relies upon machines and formulas — accumulated through centuries of culture — to perform his daily tasks, faces the realization that his allegiance to social progress and intellect-born learning will not save him. To serve a social ideal will mean nothing in a life-or-death crisis. To serve God, to serve that which no revolution can disturb, yet which is the cause and *raison d'être* of all revolutions — that is the Piscean's duty.

Transcendence, overcoming, piercing through illusions and false security, severance of social ties, embarking for the great adventure with utter faith and in denuded simplicity of being: all these things are to be learned in Pisces. Man is here face to face with himself, and with that Greater Self which he names: God. He can refuse such a confrontation. He can cling to oppressive and decadent cities. He can bundle up with refugees and moan forever before the Wailing Walls provided by dying religions and bloated social "Saviors." But then, he will be ploughed under, as manure for the spring sowings.

To renounce and to transcend means mental criticism of a sort. Mind, in the Signs preceding the equinoxes (Virgo and Pisces), is the constant critic, cutting away the crystallizations or fallacies of the past and intent upon clearing the stage for a new kind of living and realization. It is mind telling what should be forgotten, pruned away, regenerated or transcended. In Pisces, the social delusions, the exaggerated idealism, the cranky notions, the revolutionary fetishes, the scientific materialism, the civilized monstrosities which have swarmed through the Aquarian period must be cut away. Man sheds here his social vestures and stands bare before God within — that is, before the Christos, the burden of his future Destiny. Indeed, more than *social* vestures must be laid aside; for these social factors, now that the Night-force wanes, are turning not only negative but also *subjective*. The social becomes the psychic. Social dreams are transfigured into psychic phantasms; social frustrations, into subconscious complexes.

Pisces, in its negative or subjective aspect, represents the realm of the subconscious (Freud) or the personal unconscious (Jung). This personal unconscious is the end-product of all the individual's failures at adapting himself successfully to his environment — from family up to organized society, from Cancer to Capricorn. The contents of the personal unconscious are negative, because produced by a subjective defeatism which leads to self-pity and feeds the multitudinous fears constituting *inverted psychic energy*. Complexes are crystallized fears. Energy, in them, is "tied in knots" and circulates no longer. The power-filled substance of the psyche, through them, has turned slowly destructive, or at least distorting. The complex is, at times, like a concave or convex mirror which disshapes the images of living. It is psychic astigmatism. At other times, it becomes revengeful and cancerous: a growth that eats up the psycho-mental substance of consciousness and produces schizophrenia and the various kinds of manias.

In Pisces, these complexes must be faced. The confrontation may be met through understanding, through guided self-introspection (psychological analysis under a trained analyst), through the many techniques devised by Oriental *gurus*. But, in a great many cases, it implies not only an individual effort but as well a *collective* arousal, such as comes through a wave of religious fervor. This need be so, because crystallizations to be dealt with are not only caused by the individual's failure, but even more by the fallacious and atrophying traditions of family, religion and society, which impose upon the child since birth a collection of often ludicrous obstacles — some, however, unavoidable and on the whole constructive — to the spontaneous and natural flow of his energies.

Thus, it is said that the "sins of the fathers" shall visit seven generations. Our modern neuroses are likewise to be laid at the doors of the Victorian era, which in turn merely revealed the pressures and fallacies forced upon our European-Christian humanity for centuries and which only an aristocratic framework of society had kept from contaminating every man, woman and child. This framework having collapsed, the individualistic rule of the bourgeoisie, exacerbated by the release of vast powers through technology, let loose all the monsters of the subconscious. Thus, our many complexes and manias, just as the early Middle Ages — heirs to the decay of the Celtic and Roman Empires — had their *succubi* and *incubi*, their demons and their witches.

Man has to face not only his personal unconscious but also the collective unconscious of his particular race, of his particular culture. Birth in Aries means having passed through this deceitful and dark realm of racial memories, which the occultist has named the "astral world" or the "lower astral light." Rebirth in Aries means, for the mature personality, to have faced the "Guardian of the threshold" whose terrors are graphically pictured in Bulwer Lytton's famous novel *Zanoni*; and to have won in the encounter. In a positive sense, every birth means assimilating the mother's blood. The future must ever feed on the substance of the past. This past, the eternal mother, is Mary; which means etymologically, the "sea," whence all life must always spring, *whether for birth or rebirth*.

Nothing is produced vitally anew which does not emerge from the "sea." And the "sea" is Pisces, ruled by Neptune. Neptune's trident has three prongs and Pisces' zodiacal hieroglyph has also three lines. For this reason, the Gospel symbolism speaks of the three "Marys": Mary, the Mother; Mary, the love-bearer; Mary, the servant — birth, rebirth and every-day living in consecrated activity. In Pisces, the individual must go through the Eternal Feminine. This is the eternal Chrysalis, which is as nothing, yet which contains all potencies of renewal. It is the realm of metamorphosis and that of psychic glamor; the world of rapture and that of eternal mist; openness to God and mediumship to the phantasms of a decaying past; the martyr's sacrifice and the ghastly Inquisitions which feed sadistic frustrations under the mask of religious work.

Pisces must not be considered only as a Sign of social or mystical openness, with an under-meaning of passivity. In its sea-depths there is violence and storm. Severance is performed by the sword. Fanaticism is ruthless and the monk's retreat into the desert, where he can best face, in aloneness, his entire past and all the human races' memories, is a trial of courage and resilient strength. For this reason, many generals and heroes carried the zodiacal signature of Pisces in their nature. They knew how to stand still and to unfurl their energies; how to be ruthless, with themselves as with others. Pisces is aroused depth; and nothing can be more devastating than the tidal wave or the sea-born hurricane.

In Pisces, there is always something of finality, yet of expectancy. Even gentleness has undertones of mystery. There are transitions hidden in every corner of the being. There is often personal aloofness and distant nobility, as if issues were too big or too set to involve the mere personality. There is a sense of possession by an eternal unrest, on the background of which all set things appear temporary or useless. And if that mood prevails in the personality, a fatal kind of introversion slowly empties the consciousness of living contents. Men return to the ghostly world of the unconscious — perhaps as Roman Stoics living in noble aloofness while their world is destroyed, perhaps as dreamers translating all memories into phantasies, or, if afraid of psychic phantasies, building rigid intellectual systems and useless algebras to frame their hollowness with elegant arabesques.

In its highest and most spiritual aspect, Pisces reveals itself as pure compassion. Here we see the great Personage whose being is full to overflowing, because he has absorbed the wholeness of his race's experience. In his plenitude, society is mirrored and endowed with the fullest significance. And because he can go no farther, except he ascend to transcendent and formless *Nirvanas*, to him comes the great choice: solitary bliss or compassion. The former is the goal of "spiritual selfishness," sought after under the great delusion that there can be individual salvation. But the Compassionate One understands that, in reality and in truth, there can be no individual salvation. No man can rise to a Reality that is vital and significant, who does not take with him the past whence he arose. The individual can only be "saved" in that day when the whole of humanity will have reached fulfillment. Isolationism is the only sin that life cannot forgive, because he who conveniently forgets the rungs of the ladder which helped him to reach the pinnacle, leaves a mark upon life which nothing and no one can eradicate but himself.

Compassion is the absolute Law of a universe in which there is order and harmony. Compassion is the heart of reality, because reality is based on the experience of *organic wholeness*, and he who truly experiences all things as organic wholes cannot fail to see himself as part of some Greater Whole, however much he may have attained integral wholeness in his own being. In Pisces, therefore, the "Messenger from the Divine City" meets the men whom it is his burden of destiny to teach and to impregnate with the Glad Tidings of the New Life. Should he recoil in dismay before the picture of decay and materialism which a crumbling civilization presents, he would then fail his true destiny.

The burden of Pisces is that one should not recoil before anything, low and horrible as it might be, on the basis of one's own purity and excellence; that one should move on toward the common plains with arms and soul laden with the significance and glory of the hills "whence come salvation." The "Cedar of Lebanon" must willingly let itself be cut, that houses may be built for the homeless, that ships may sail to lands of riches, that "Temples of Solomon" may become, in fact, dwelling places of God among men.

In Pisces, the "Divine City," that is far and beyond, can be erected, in reality and in significance, among men.

This is the end of the cycle, which bears within its vital depths the beginnings of the New Life. The Day-force and the Night-force have come once more to the point of equilibrium. What is to become "initiated" is no longer, as it was at the threshold of Libra, the individual; it is now Humanity, as an organic whole. And this is the last blessing of the closing cycle, the eternal promise of all cyclic consummation: that the constant dualism of ever-changing life can be integrated in organic wholes ceaselessly more encompassing, through the creative behavior of Personalities ever more compassionate and more deeply integrated; that Day and Night may be realized as the two complementary poles of life and consciousness, in moments of human perception so lucid and so rich with universal contents that such illuminations may remain as beacon lights to be guidance and joy to ever vaster reaches of life. It is the promise of eternal rebirth, which leaves nothing unredeemed and excludes no one; the promise of the everlasting and timeless Presence of God in the man who fully welcomes the total integration of all that brought him to his present consummation; in whom, therefore, is accomplished the synthesis of past and future in the fullness and glory of moments that are the "eternal Now."

Chapter Three

The Creative Release of Spirit

To and fro, the heart of reality beats. To and fro, the Day-force and the Night-force weave their patterns of organic relationship in rhythmic interplay. But Man is neither systole nor diastole, neither the work of the day nor the dream-activity of the night. Man is the field in which the battle of the two streams of energies proceeds unceasingly in alternation of defeat and victory — or else, man is the integrated and creative whole within which the two polarities of human experience, balancing one another in dynamic harmony, contribute constantly to the activity of the creative wholeness of that whole which uses them.

In the first of these two conditions, man operates as a *nature-conditioned* being, and his life and experience constantly oscillate between consciousness and unconsciousness, individual and collective, life and death, rebirth and once more death. In the second state, man is a *Spirit-conditioned* being, an utterance of destiny, yet deeply rooted in silence. He is poised in a harmony of opposites which both transcends these opposites and includes all their manifestations.

The term "nature-conditioned" being may refer to a personality operating at the level of instincts and in a state of preponderant unconscious activity; or it may describe a person with great intellectual powers, priding himself in that his behavior is ruled by rational and ethical standards deliberately accepted and applied. In both cases, nevertheless, the human being will have to be considered as a "nature conditioned" being, because he is in fact conditioned by the alternation of negative and positive, of *plus* and *minus* — his moods and feelings, his thoughts and his interests waxing and waning, pulled hither and thither by the rhythmic interplay of the two great forces of nature.

If the man lives according to his instincts, then his rhythm of change will closely follow the rhythm of life-phenomena on this earth; he will act as a seasonal creature. If he functions predominantly as a civilized and intellectually conscious person, the basic rhythms of earth-nature will be overladen with counter-rhythms produced by social rules of behavior, by the demands of city-life, and by his own conscious and unconscious reactions to the impulsions which sway his physical and psychological organism. However, to oppose the rhythm of nature is still to live under its sway, for one is as much bound by that against which one rebels as by that to which one is subservient.

Even the attempt willfully to control the great cosmic forces of life and to set deliberate patterns for their manifestations within the human personality is still a mark of subordination to the powers which the will tries to canalize and to tame. The energies which may be controlled in one direction and at one time will always tend to rebound with increased strength in some other direction, at some other time. And he who becomes, by sheer conscious determination, a poem of pure light, releases the very forces which, in the opposite direction, will congregate around a manifestation of equally "pure" darkness. Dualism will thus be intensified; it will not be solved. Intensification may be a necessary phase in the global attainment of spiritual living; for it is said that the "lukewarm" represent the lowest state of being — yet the quality of Spirit-conditioned being is not really reached by stressing to the limit one pole of life. It is not produced by the triumph of the characteristics of one of the two forces after bestowing upon these characteristics the qualification of "good."

The first requirement which is to be met by a person reaching toward a condition of Spirit-conditioned activity is that he should consciously and understandingly include and accept all the manifestations of the Day-force and the Night-force, of the individual and the collective polarities of life. As he does so consistently, a time necessarily comes when the two forces, periodically waxing and waning, reach a point of balance within his cycle of being. At that moment, the person who, until then, had been polarized at any time by the force then dominant, finds himself equally swayed by the two forces. Their pulls neutralize each other. The man, as a whole, becomes still. In that incredibly brief moment of stillness and "silence," the whole can express its wholeness without being controlled by the nature of one of the forces playing through it. In that moment, the wholeness of all that occurs during the entire cycle is revealed in a synthesis of being which transcends the qualities produced by the ever-changing and ever-challenged preponderance of either the Day or Night forces. Nature is transcended; Spirit is revealed.

Spirit is wholeness of cyclic activity; and that wholeness is dispassionate and even in its quality of being, because it includes the complementary energies in a balanced state. Such a "balanced state" occurs in the yearly cycle of the Day-force and the Night-force at the equinoxes. Thus, these two points in the yearly cycle are the *archetypal symbols of those moments in any life-cycle at which Spirit can be revealed.*

In *any* life-cycle, however small or however vast, these two equinoctial points are the "gates of Initiation" which mark the entrance into the realm of Spirit-conditioned being. That realm can be entered from the side of the particularizing Day-force or from that of the universalizing Night-force. But at the Spring equinox the experience of Spirit cannot be normally *held* in consciousness, because the personality-structure, which alone could hold it, is not yet formed. At the Fall equinox it is the individual personality which takes the initiatory step, in conscious self-surrender to the Night-force; and in compensation for that surrender, it can retain a structural memory of the event. It can gain personal immortality in Spirit, and henceforth operate as a Spirit-conditioned being.

The first condition necessary to become prepared for such an equinoctial confrontation is *an understanding of the cyclic nature of all experience*. No experience can have spiritual meaning unless it is referred to the wholeness of the cycle in which it occurs. The "reference" may be instinctive or intuitional, below or above the level of the normal consciousness; but because all experience begins in the realm of change and thus of time, the spiritualization of experience implies that the entire cycle to which the experience naturally belongs has to be seen and felt

THE CREATIVE RELEASE OF SPIRIT 133

in that particular experience. The wholeness of the cycle must be realized by the experiencer within the "equinoctial" experience which can be made into a focal point for the expression of the wholeness of the entire cycle.

Because at the "equinoctial" points of any cycle the two forces, the interplay of which is the substance of the cycle, are balanced and neutralized, in that equinoctial moment the wholeness of the whole cycle can become *active*. This activity is essentially different from the activity which is conditioned by a preponderance of either the Day-force or the Night-force, of individual or collective. It is Spirit-conditioned activity: *creative* activity. The creative power of Spirit potentially radiates from the core of the equilibratedness of the two forces. It is a power which makes all things new. It is sheer originality. It is the incalculable element which upsets predictions based on sequences of cause and effect. It produces an activity which is not conditioned by causation or by time-relationship — even though it is released at a certain moment of the cycle. It is activity *which creates time and starts a new causal sequence*. It is activity which is free.

What is implied in the foregoing is nothing less than a technique for becoming acquainted with the timing of the manifestations of this creative Spirit; also, for preparing oneself consciously to meet these moments of equilibrium during which the *possibility* of Spirit-conditioned activity is present. A possibility — not a certainty. Moments of unstable and dynamic equilibrium come according to the law of cyclic and polar change, but these moments do not last; and unless man faces them with awakened consciousness there can be for him no experience of Spirit-conditioned activity. The "gates" open, but he who has fallen asleep while passing in front of the gates does not *experience* the vision which the gates reveal; for experience presupposes consciousness of a sort in a more or less individualized experiencer.

Spirit can, and does, act whether there is consciousness or not. But where there is, as yet, no formed structures of personality to experience it consciously, the activity of Spirit operates in the darkness of the realm of Roots, where sunlight does not reach. It operates through the instincts, through channels of direct, but unconscious, expression — and this is symbolically the Spring equinox, Aries. Where, on the other hand, a conscious and formed personality has been built (through the symbolical six-month process at work from Aries to the end of Virgo), the creative activity of Spirit operates in terms of conscious realizations within the expectant total organism of man. It releases, then, Meaning. It operates, symbolically speaking, as the Seed at the Fall equinox, Libra.

The higher function of astrology, known to mystics of all ages and all races, is to reveal to the evolving personality the Seed-moments of his cyclic experience: those equinoctial moments during which Spirit can act within the human soul in terms of new cosmic Impulses or of creative Meaning. Such moments are revealed in a number of ways. In a universally human sense, they are the seasonal turning points of the year when the Sun actually and concretely crosses the thresholds of Aries and Libra. At such times, the whole of nature — terrestrial and human — receives a Visitation of the creative Spirit. They constitute days of maximum potentiality — for birth or rebirth, for emotional outgoings or sacramental self-offerings to

THE CREATIVE RELEASE OF SPIRIT   135

the community, for building or transfiguring the forms of our human experience. And such spiritual openings were celebrated by rituals in ancient civilizations which were close to the pulse of seasonal life.

There are, however, other kinds of astrological cycles which can reveal to us the existence of similar moments of release of Spirit; cycles produced by the periodical motions of two celestial bodies in reference to the experiencer on this Earth. Of these cycles, the lunation cycle is the foremost. It is the cycle which refers to the regular sequence of New Moons and Full Moons. In this cycle, two factors — Sun and Moon — are also seen in their ever-changing periodical interplay, and four basic moments stand out as climactic points of the cycle. These manifest as the four phases of the Moon.

In the case of such cycles, what is measured is the *degree of relatedness* of the two moving bodies. This relatedness, in reference to the observer on Earth, has a maximum value at the New Moon and the Full Moon; a minimum value at the First and Last Quarters. Briefly said, New Moon (the point of *conjunction*) corresponds to the Spring equinox; Full Moon (the point of *opposition*), to the fall equinox — this, because the equinoxes are also the moments of the year cycle when the Day-force and the Night-force are *most closely associated in man's experience*. The New Moon is thus a point at which creative Spirit is released as instinct or form-building energy. At the Full Moon, man can reach a maximum of awareness of the meaning of life-experiences. It is thus the time consecrated to the meditating Buddha.

Whenever the motions of two planets are considered in relation to an observer on the Earth, a cycle similar to the lunation cycle can be defined. The four climactic, or "crucial," moments of the cycle are the times of conjunction, of opposition and of square aspects. Here, again, conjunction is the Root-point at which the new cyclic impulse is released; and opposition, the Seed-point at which the meaning of the cyclic relationship can be reached by the consciousness *actively prepared to receive the illumination of the Spirit.*

Such cycles of planetary relationship are particularly significant when the two planets thus associated are "polar opposites." Pairs of planetary opposites are: Mars (positive) and Venus (negative) — Jupiter and Mercury — Saturn and the Moon — and, in a sense at least, Uranus and the Sun. Thus, whenever Mars and Venus are in opposition in the sky, men should seek to fathom the meaning of their emotional, personal nature. When the Moon opposes Saturn, every month, the moment is propitious for an effort in consciousness aiming at liberation from the *Karma* (causal sequence) of past events. At the times of conjunction, the entire organism should be aligned to receive the new impulse to activity. Thus, a conjunction of Jupiter and Mercury is of great moment in establishing a new foundation for mental activity.

These cycles have effect in the lives of all men. Beside them, personal cycles may be analyzed which deal with the "progressed positions" of the planets in an individual chart. The same meaning applies to such cycles, but in a strictly personal manner. For instance, the oppositions of the progressed Moon to progressed (or radical) Saturn are very significant indications of times in the life of an individual when he can step out of the "circle of necessity." In a less definite manner, the cycles of any two planets can also be

THE CREATIVE RELEASE OF SPIRIT 137

considered; for wherever there is periodical oscillation and rhythm, wherever the pulse of life is felt, within the compass of such cyclic alternation of positive and negative emphases there are moments in which an unstable equilibrium between positive and negative is reached. These are the moments of release for That which transcends the everlasting interplay of opposites, the realm of time and change.

Such a transcendence, however, is not absolute. We do not postulate here a realm of timeless Spirit absolutely distinct from that of cyclic change. Spirit is transcendent only in the sense that the quality of wholeness is transcendent to the nature of the parts of the whole. Wherever there is cyclic change, only parts change. The wholeness of the whole is constant — in what we might call another dimension of being. It is only in the realm of parts that the cyclic interplay of "individual" and "collective" occurs.

Change occurs *within* the whole. There are times when the force of individualization, or personification, pulls each part away from the others and tends to give it the character of a whole — a character which, obviously, it never attains absolutely. Then there are times when the force of collectivization, or group integration, pulls all the parts together, emphasizing in each the sense of their commonness of being, and the will to sacrifice their existence for the sake of the whole. But there are also two moments in every cycle — however small the cycle may be — when the two pulls become equal.

In most cases, nothing happens as this equalization occurs, because the equilibrium reached lasts only a split-second and the momentum of the two forces carries them past the point of balance. Yet in a few instances a *structure of consciousness* has been built beforehand, which catches the flash that is released at the exact point of equilibrium. In that flash, the wholeness of the whole acts upon the part which had in readiness the structure of consciousness necessary to serve as a base for that action of the wholeness of the whole. This action is Spirit in operation. It is the creative factor.

Individual and *collective* are in constant cyclic interplay in the realm of parts; and that interplay produces a kind of activity in which there is the inevitability and the compulsive fate which are born of the causal sequence of action and reaction. But in the activity in which the wholeness of the whole operates as *creative* Spirit, there is unpredictability and originality, and from it flows a sense of freedom.

This creative activity of Spirit operates in every man who has built the instrumentality through which it can function. It operates in and through a particular person; yet it does not belong to that person. Its source is the wholeness of that whole in which human organisms "live and have their being"; and the whole is, primarily, Humanity. Every man moves within the sphere of Humanity; partly as an exemplar of generically and collectively human traits, partly as one struggling toward a state of individualized personality. The complementary tides of individualism and collectivism ever sway the myriads of men who, in their Root-origin as in their Seed-togetherness, constitute the "greater whole," Humanity. And the wholeness of that whole is "Man."

Wherever the pulse of life is felt, there must be disequilibrium, conflict, strain and the experience of suffering. But there are those who have become, through their own efforts as "builders of personality" and through their understanding of cyclic rhythms, vehicles for the creative action of "Man." Because they have succeeded in taking advantage of moments of cyclic equilibrium, because they have been awake and ready when the equinoctial gates open, they have become identified with "Man."

As there are cycles which take millions of years for their completion, so there are cycles which last only seconds of time and much less than a second. To him who can feel the rhythm of those infinitesimally small cycles, there are always and forever equinoxes. In and through him the Spirit is released as an electrical alternative current which is Root and which is Seed — which builds universes of form and releases conscious meanings, whence again shall be born new forms. He is Root and he is Seed, and so swiftly both, that time no longer exists. He has become, at once, both equinoxes. He has become, at once, the entire Zodiac. He is free. The wholeness of the Whole creates eternally through him in an everlasting act of Incarnation.

ABOUT THE AUTHOR (1973)

Dane Rudhyar is probably the most widely respected astrologer today, but he is also a philosopher, poet, novelist, composer, painter and aesthetic theoretician. Born in Paris in 1895, he came to America late in 1916. The next year his musical compositions were performed in New York along with works by Erik Satie and other French composers in the first performance of dissonant polytonal music in America. He became interested in astrology in 1920 and combined this interest with studies of Eastern philosophies and, after 1930, the psychology of Carl Jung. His widely acclaimed book The Astrology of Personality was originally published in 1936 and reissued in paperback in 1970. Since 1933 Rudhyar has written extensively for astrological publications and has published more than a dozen books in which he has developed a "humanistic" approach to the ancient science. In March 1972, radio station KPFA in San Francisco celebrated Rudhyar's seventy-seventh birthday with a retrospective of his work. His piano compositions have recently been performed from coast to coast and are now available in records. He is a popular lecturer and maintains an energetic schedule of appearances throughout the country.

RUDHYAR AUDIO ARCHIVES

Listen to archival recordings of astrology lectures with Dane Rudhyar at: https://www.astrologyuniversity.com/rudhyar-audio-archives/

ADDITIONAL TITLES BY RAVEN DREAMS PRESS

An Astrological Mandala by Dane Rudhyar

Healing the Soul: Pluto, Uranus and the Lunar Nodes by Mark Jones

The Soul Speaks: The Therapeutic Potential of Astrology by Mark Jones

The Planetary Nodes and Collective Evolution by Mark Jones

The Astrological Moon by Darby Costello

Earth & Air by Darby Costello

Water & Fire by Darby Costello

Cycles of Light: Exploring the Mysteries of Solar Returns by Lynn Bell

Soul Path Way: The Dance of Astrology, Intuition and Spiritual Awakening by Kay Taylor

A Cosmic Dialogue: Reassessing Methods for Understanding New Planets by Patricia Garner